HORIZON FEVER II

Explorer A.E.Filby's own account of his extraordinary Australasian adventures, 1921 - 1931

ARCHIBALD EDMUND FILBY

Collated by
VICTORIA TWEAD & JOE TWEAD

Copyright © Text, 2021 by Victoria Twead

Photographs © Victoria Twead

Available in Hardback Paperback, Large Print and Ebook

Hardback ISBN: 978-1-922476-42-5

Paperback ISBN: 978-1-922476-29-6

Large Print Paperback ISBN: 978-1-922476-43-2

Large Print Hardback ISBN: 978-1-922476-44-9

Ebook: 978-1-922476-46-3

Formatted by Ant Press

Published by Antpress.org

All rights reserved.

No part of this book may be reproduced in any form or by any electronic or mechanical means, including information storage and retrieval systems, without written permission from the author, except for the use of brief quotations in a book review.

Archibald Edmund Filby
Born 1900 - Died 1942

CONTENTS

FREE Photo Book	vii
1. Uncle Archie	1
2. The Horizon Chaser	7
3. Royal Mail Ship Orsova	11
4. Australia	17
5. Life in Australia	25
6. An ill-fated expedition through the wilds of south-west Australia.	31
7. Tally Ho! The Tallyman. A Narrow Squeak.	35
8. The Taming of a Tartar	37
9. Bell's Bonza Buckjumping Broncos and Bullocks	43
10. The Donkey Race for Boys	51
11. Trekking	55
12. Camp-Fire Tales	59
13. Trekking, Continued	63
14. Still Trekking	67
15. From Trekking to Photography	71
16. From Photography to Hunting	75
17. From Hunter to Actor	77
18. From Actor to Hotel Representative	81
19. From Hotel Representative to Realty Development	85
20. Touring in Northern Queensland	87
21. A Visit to Tasmania (1925)	99
22. A Remarkable Adventure by Motor Combination	103
23. A Duel with Sabres on Thursday Island	107
24. By Sailing Lugger through the Pacific	109
25. A Glorious Expedition	113
26. Three Months on the Island of Ceylon	117
27. Borneo and Sarawak	119
28. Java	121
29. Oriental Ways	125
30. More Pearl Diving and I visit Bali	129

31. Tiger! Tiger!	133
32. Motor Business in the Far East	137
33. India	147
34. Hindoo	153
35. Singapore, India, Burma [Myanmar], Thailand and China	155
36. Through Persia, Iraq and back to the United Kingdom	163
Epilogue	167
A Request…	169
So what happened next?	171
About Victoria Twead	173
Ant Press Online	179

FREE PHOTO BOOK
TO BROWSE OR DOWNLOAD

❦

For photographs and additional unpublished material to accompany this book, browse or download the

FREE PHOTO BOOK
from
www.victoriatwead.com/free-stuff

I

UNCLE ARCHIE

Archibald Edmund Filby, proclaimed 'the World's most travelled motorist', was my uncle. He died before I was born but I eventually inherited a manuscript titled *Horizon Fever*, a record of Archie's return trip, between London and Cape Town, undertaken at the start of 1931 and concluding in 1935.

My brother, Philip, inherited 14 additional scrapbooks that had been collated by my grandfather, known to all as Solly. These were a record of Archie's youth and his travels around the world. The books were titled, 'Australia Calling', 'Asia Calling' and 'Africa Calling', each labeled according to his travel destinations. He also described his seven trips through the Sahara whilst exploring Africa.

I, and my husband, Joe, had already collated and published *Horizon Fever*. Joe suggested that Philip's additional material might also be published in separate volumes. However, unlike *Horizon Fever*, the books required a great deal more preparation before being presented to a reading public.

Horizon Fever II, Australasia Calling, details Archie's early years and travels in Australia and the Far East. *Horizon Fever III, My Seven Crossings of the Sahara,* has been completed too.

Accompanying photo books for all three books, *Horizon Fever*,

Horizon Fever II, and *Horizon Fever III* can be downloaded free of charge from my Web Page www.victoriatwead.com/free-stuff.

The illustrations/photographs were scattered across Solly's scrapbooks and Joe spent many hours scouring them for inclusion in the photo book.

As with *Horizon Fever*, I make no apologies for the quality of the photographs. Apart from a few they are all Archie's, snapped nearly a hundred years ago, some even older. One can only imagine the difficulties he encountered whilst recording his travels and using primitive camera equipment.

Having said that, he did spend a few months as a professional photographer but decided to chuck it in to continue with his travels. Some of the captions are Archie's own. Any captions (or comments) that are ours are enclosed within square brackets [thus].

Archie's adventures include every mode of motorised (and unmotorised) transport. Driving cars, riding motorbikes, and even piloting aeroplanes, are regular occurrences during his travels. He was also adept as a horse-back rider and appeared in carnivals as a bronco-rider. When and where he acquired the skills to master these is unknown but, that he did, is certain.

Attitudes in those days were very different and often shocking. Despite this, Archie's affection and respect for the indigenous populace cannot be disputed. He was clearly fascinated by the languages, customs and cultures of the peoples he encountered. In his own words, "The study of the Wild man in his Homeland is, to me, a joy."

I cannot disguise the fact that Archie enjoyed hunting and killed animals that posed little threat. He boasts, for example, the hunting of possums, animals that are more endearing than deserving of a bullet. In his defence, attitudes towards wildlife, just after The Great War, were very different to those of today.

Very few changes have been made to the original manuscript. It is as Archie typed it in the 1930's, undoubtedly at the behest of his newly-wedded wife, Miss Fay Taylor, also a writer, whom he met following a radio broadcast he made from London. More details of their relationship can be found in the Epilogue.

My apologies if the narrative sometimes appears to be disjointed. The descriptions, anecdotes and tales do not always follow an obvious time-line. Joe and I have made every effort to separate his various travels in Australia and the Far East but sometimes it has been difficult to pin-point exact dates of his activities. He often re-visits places he has been to and describes yet another set of adventures without stating exactly when they occurred.

Nevertheless I hope this does not detract from what I believe to be an interesting and, I believe, historical, account of a young man who wanted to visit all of Australasia, during the 1920's, and was unstinting in his efforts to do so.

My Uncle Archie, the eldest of three children (one of whom was my father) was born on April 18th in 1899. He was always a seeker after adventure and didn't hesitate in joining the newly-inaugurated Scouting Movement as a member of The Third Bromley Boys' Scouts.

His sense of adventure would have him, just four years later (and unbeknown to his parents), applying to serve in the British Army during the Great War. Although he gave his age as 19, he was in fact only 14. He soon found himself amongst the legitimately-aged young men of The Royal Queen's Own West Kent Regiment.

He must have seen some action but, when the fighting was fiercest, was often dispatched to fetch imaginary supplies from behind the lines. Perhaps his comrades, more observant of his true age than the recruiters had been, could not bear to see so young a life cut off in its prime.

He was educated at Saint Dunstan's College, London, before being recruited by Boots The Chemist a few months prior to the beginning of The Great War. When hostilities ended manpower understandably was scarce and anyone having a job to return to was given permission to do so. Thus Archie was granted an early discharge from His Majesty's Forces.

However, he did not stay long at Boots and his adventurous nature soon sought alternatives to what he considered to be 'the mundane work' of a chemist. Initially he turned his hand to the maintenance and selling of motor vehicles. Following a chance meeting with an American army buddy, Captain Sydney (Syd) Whitaker, they decided to pursue adventures further afield.

They were made aware of a government scheme whereby young men were invited to move to and work in Australia. Archie thought this an ideal opportunity to visit that country as well as others in the Far East. He and Syd (whom he called 'Whitty') were accepted and shipped off to the antipodes.

He carried with him the following letter of introduction:

The Rookery.
Bromley Common.
KENT.
Telephone: Bromley 1103
September 6 1920

I understand that Mr Filby is shortly proceeding to Australia, and I write this on the chance that it may be of use to him there.
Mr Archibald Filby, the bearer of this, is a member of a family which has carried on business in Bromley for at least two generations - his Father and late Grandfather have been well known to me and my predecessors during the whole of that period of over 50 years, and have been held in the highest esteem by my own family, as well as by other residents in the town and neighbourhood.
Mr A. E. Filby is 21 years of age, was educated at St Dunstan's College, Catford, and served in the late War from 1914 onwards - He belonged previously to a troop of Boy Scouts, and did valuable work in several Parliamentary elections.
(Signed)
A Norman MA JP

Archie would spend the better part of a decade exploring Australasia and would also meet his future bride, Fay Taylor, who, at the time, was a girl of sixteen and living with her parents in Singapore.

An odd incident occurred during his stay in Australia. He was arrested and charged with stealing a motorcycle and received a three month custodial sentence with hard labour. Archie makes no mention of it in any of his writings. I asked the present-day Queensland authorities for more information but they were reluctant to divulge many details. However, we have included a photocopy of his criminal record and 'mug shots' in the photo book, which also informs us that he carried out his sentence as he did not pay the fine or provide surety.

Despite having never met my Uncle, I believe his spirit lives on through his own accounts of his travels. He comes across as a courageous, feisty, quick-tempered, bossy little man, but full of fun, generous and never one to bear a grudge. I imagine his companions found him difficult to travel with, but he made friends easily and was much in demand by the Press and for radio and early television broadcasts.

One final thought, Archie had little money. He worked his way around the world, doing whatever caught his fancy, always seeking adventure. Undoubtedly the malaria that later took his life in Sierra Leone, in 1943, was contracted whilst touring the Far East and India in particular.

And so, without further ado, as before, I hand over the story-telling to my Uncle Archie.

Victoria Twead
July 2019

2

THE HORIZON CHASER

The years 1914 to 1918 saw me in the British Forces. This, no doubt, whetted my appetite for finding out what was lying on the other side of the Horizon.

During a visit home on leave, Armistice was declared and I called at the Hotel Cecil which was head Office for the Flying Corps. I remembered that a Police Notice described me as a fluent talker and this gift I now employed and, rather to my astonishment, I found myself discharged.

Although I still had about four years to serve of my apprenticeship with Messrs Boots Chemists and Druggists of Nottingham, I had other ideas. Following several shots at various jobs, and after a really considerable waste of time, I found myself selling motor cycles and lorries which came from the Army Disposal Board. This I did with an old army friend of mine, Captain Syd Whitaker.

In charge of the Army Disposal Board was a man whom we knew and a man we had never met. There was a keen demand for our goods and we had only to walk down Great Portland Street [London] to make excellent profits quickly. Like all good things it came to an end and in a simple way.

I sold a batch of Triumphs to be delivered on Monday. This

happened to be a Bank Holiday and the watchman at our stores, thinking to do me a good turn, sold some of the machines and was unable to give delivery. This led to enquiries and our colleague on the Disposal Board was removed from his job. We then got no more lorries or motor cycles through.

At the time I was living at the Overseas Officers Club in St James Square. [Washington Inn American YMCA.] The constant flow of officers through its portals made it a very lively place. Whitty and I (almost permanent residents) were in great demand and many were the wild nights we had in the good company that hailed from all parts of the British Empire.

I recollect The Old Palace Royal where I arranged with the head waiter to settle all drinks-bills the next morning, thereby giving incontestable proof to our acquaintances of our high standing in London. This waiter could also be depended upon to supply any number of well dressed ladies to help enliven proceedings, especially party nights.

Whitty and I decided to tour England on motor cycles. These we had to buy back at a high price from our previous customers. The start was inauspicious for my companion, who had not ridden a cycle for many years, and charged into a traffic cop at London Bridge.

After many apologies and references about having just been discharged from the Army, he got away with it, only to make a false start and charge the policeman in the rear. The officer sternly ordered us to go back home, which kind advice we adopted while the going was good.

At the Club I met the Director of The Ray Motor Company who were bringing a new model out. They had heard of our successful sales and he offered me the position of Sales Manager. Nearly twenty years old and full of confidence, I accepted immediately. [Contract states 3 March 1920 at £500pa.] Whitty was appointed Assistant Manager and business promised to loom big. We found however that at that date only one experimental machine had been constructed.

For some weeks the firm paid our salaries but I decided to run over to Paris to interview the man who was financing the show. I stayed at a hotel with the designer and his wife. After a lengthy discussion I eventually agreed to accept three months salary (on the spot) in lieu of notice. I never looked for a job in England again.

Then in conversation with Beverly Baxter (Secretary to Lord Beaverbrook) I was impressed with his glowing account of the great possibilities to be exploited in the antipodes. He followed up his description by presenting me with a large-brimmed green stetson hat which he won off Beaverbrook at tennis. [Lord Beaverbrook was a newspaper magnate and politically influential in the UK during the first half of the 20th Centaury. Beverley Baxter was the editor of Lord Beaverbrook's newspaper, the *Daily Express*.]

Whitty now got in touch with one of the Overseas Settlements Organisations who agreed that we were the right type. They gave us our passage tickets and funds for expenses and congratulated us on our public spirit in assisting the government scheme.

No time was lost and soon we were on the Orient liner *Orsova* which sailed from Tilbury, bound for Australia. There were a number of other officers, all seeking their fortunes in the antipodes. I would like to mention that we had one of the most elaborate send-offs it would be possible to imagine from the Club and Hotels. Our presents were really embarrassing in quantity and quality.

3

ROYAL MAIL SHIP ORSOVA

The world opened up a new vista for me when I stepped on board The Royal Mail Ship *Orsova* berthed in the Tilbury Docks. We were outward bound for Australia! Fog, cold, rain and darkness were the chief features just then. The date was 27th November 1920.

After disposing of our overland trunks and numerous cabin boxes and bags, I inspected the ship with my travelling companion, Captain Syd Whitaker. We agreed that it was a fine liner and that we should have a good voyage.

Our sleeping berths were first class. We knew we should put our tired heads on those lovely pillows and dream of golden sunshine, golden plains and the golden future which was soon to be ours. Everything augured for real success: we were young and strong.

We had first class equipment, a considerable amount of the needful cash in our banking account, supplemented by a generous Government grant for services rendered during the Great War. After much leave takings, and many promises, we sailed away on the high tide of life.

Dropping the pilot, we reached Ushant, then Cape Finisterre, Cape St Vincent and Tarifa, landing at Gibraltar at 3.30pm December 1st. We raced ashore and explored the wonders of that remarkable Rock.

Gibraltar is two square miles and its civil population of 1700 souls is comprised of mostly Spanish and Italians. The Naval Works are considerable and 70 acres were reclaimed from the sea. The Anchorage within stone moles extend to 500 acres alone. Throughout The Rock are extensive galleries and elaborate systems of tunnels.

The Governor and Commander in Chief is General Sir Edmund Ironside. [Archie is mistaken. At the time he visited Gibralta (December 1920) the Governor was Sir Horace Smith-Dorrien. General Sir Edmund Ironside was the Governor from August 1938 until July 1939.]

Once under Moorish rule, in 1704 it was captured by Sir George Rooke and during the American War of Independence withstood a siege by the French and Spanish combined. It was taken over by Great Britain in 1738 under the Treaty of Versailles. I was delighted and pleasantly astonished at this my first visit. Little did I think then that I would return there again and again both for business and pleasure.

It struck me as curious that, in such a cosmopolitan place, everyone spoke English. Also the rule of the road was 'keep right' - probably the only British possession where this rule obtains.

Time and tide waits for no man and we continued past Cape Gata, San Antonio and San Sabaston. Calling at Toulon we spent some hours in that interesting town. We awoke next morning to find ourselves in the lovely bay of Naples.

A full day's sightseeing and shopping was put in at the famous town of Naples. Everyone felt satisfied that good use had been taken of that call, where months could have been profitably spent exploring such a glorious place.

Leaving Crete on our starboard we put into Port Said [Egypt] on December 9th: a very primitive place. The shops and cafes were opened on the arrival of any vessel and closed again on its departure, whether it be day or night.

After a skirmish around the bazaars, and sampling the wines of Africa, we carried on to Suez where we stopped for 60 minutes. We were not permitted to land, so of course we did. We raced back, out of breath, to the warning accompaniment of the ship's siren and surplus steam from the Captain on the bridge. At any rate we had explored the Dark Continent.

Jebel Teir was next then we sailed through the Straits of Perim. On December 14th we steamed by Aden, or I should say 'boiled by'. Our overcoats and woollies, which we had clasped round us so tightly only two weeks before, had long been peeled off and we now boiled in the tropical heat. Passing Cape Guardfui and Minnikoi we reached Colombo and explored the fascinating Island of Ceylon [Sri Lanka].

On Christmas Day we 'Crossed The Line' [Equator] off Keeling Island. The crew, ably assisted by the passengers, staged an elaborate burlesque, and I was not able to distinguish which was more popular, Father Neptune, the old God of The Seas, or Father Christmas. There was more fun, joy, feasting, and drinking crowded into that 24 hours than was humanly possible.

It was 28th December 1920 when we landed at Fremantle, the 'Gateway' to the Australian Continent from Europe, Asia, and Africa. One wonders what the old mariner Captain Fremantle of *HMS Challenger* would now think of the tree lined Swan River, where he hoisted the British Flag in 1829, had he been alive today. This busy seaport also has services running to Singapore, Java, and in fact practically all Overseas Liners touch here.

We briefly stepped ashore to make a number of calls and also telephoned various people. Then we took the train to Perth. Rushing back again to board our *Orsova*, we continued our voyage and found a sprinkling of new passengers taking the place of some pals who had disembarked.

We had seen so much and done so much that it seemed ages since we left the hospitable Washington Inn at St James Square in London. Then there had been all the good-byes, and fond and sad leave takings at Tilbury. We thought of wonderful Gibraltar, the mountains of lights of all colours; the reflections round the black rock base, then Ceylon!

We next made the fair City of Adelaide. "Be sure you see the Town Hall," we were told.

There is a story that it was built by convicts, and the architect was promised liberty for his services. [Despite the possibility of a 'good story', we found no evidence that it was built or designed by convicts.]

A reference to a map of Australia will disclose its immensity. The smallest Continent and the world's largest Island! There is a line commencing at 34 degrees latitude and 139 degrees longitude [at Adelaide] called Goyder's Line of Rainfall. Districts north of this have an average rainfall of less than 8 inches.

Some months later I had the curious experience in a part where the rainfall was so scanty that, on the occasion of a heavy rain, the children rushed about terrified as they had never seen rain before.

The land in the South East is so rich that almost anything will grow well there. Until lately it was quite inaccessible from Adelaide. There were only two surveyed roads, one through 8 miles [13 km] of desert with an unmade track along the railway; the other along the coast through a series of Salt Lakes called the Coorong. In winter this track was impassable. In summer it was so rough that it took a week to do the 312 miles from Adelaide to Mount Gambier in the south east.

Then on to Melbourne where we said adieu to the good old Orient Liner *Orsova* after a most glorious and happy trip. The 14,000 mile voyage had taken 50 days.

We then struck out to explore the Continent of our adoption. We were met by Mrs Bell, an aunt of my travelling pal, Syd Whitaker. She informed us that her son, Mr Curly Bell, had been called away to Queensland but he would telephone us later and go into a scheme with us. We put up at the Port Phillip Club Hotel (Melbourne) for a few days and then went up to Geelong, Victoria.

One evening while walking along Moorabool Street I noticed a lamp notifying that a Lodge of Oddfellows was being held there. Being a Member of the Manchester Unity, I rapped the signal on the door, then gave the Pass Word and Sign. I was quite taken back by the warmth of the welcome I received from my Brethren in the antipodes. I also received good helpful advice, invites, and offers of jobs galore had I wanted them.

[Archie was presented with the following letter of introduction from the Geelong Oddfellows Lodge.]

Loyal Geelong Lodge, No. 4257
Manchester Unity

Independent Order of Oddfellows
Manchester Unity Hall
Moorabool Street
GEELONG, 11/7 1921
Secretary
JAS. CLARKE
KILGOUR STREET EAST
Telephone No. 2214

To Whom it may Concern

Dear Sir and Bro

The Bearer Bro A. E. Filby is a financial member of the Loyal Ratcliffe Lodge No 7486 England. He is fully paid up to September 1921 and has brought out with him the necessary introduction from his Lodge as he is now travelling in Queensland.
I commend him to your care and any kindness that may be shown to him will be reciprocated by the Officers and members of the above Lodge as well as his own should an opportunity occur.

With Fraternal Greetings
I am
Yours Fraternally
Jas Clarke (Signature)

A few days later I called upon the The Honourable Lord Forster of Lepe, the Governor General of Australia. [The Governor General's official residence is Government House, Canberra.]

He gave me a hearty welcome to the Dominion. He enquired about Home, the Family, and the Town of our birth, that is Bromley, Kent. He said he knew my grandparents best.

He introduced me to Lieutenant Norman, his aid-de-camp (from Bromley Common) and after a merry chat and handshake they wished me the best of fortune.

"You will make good, it's a fine country" said Lord Forster.

I replied, "Thank you, sir but I'm afraid I am a rolling stone. You know, gathers no moss?"

"Ah!" Lord Forster said with a laugh. "It should produce a fine polish."

Whitty and I visited the Houses of Parliament at Canberra. They certainly are a very fine pile.

4

AUSTRALIA

We took a train to Sydney and spent a week exploring the City. Sydney harbour has one of the largest Bridge spans in the world. The whole structure reminds me of Tower Bridge, London, but instead of the upper thoroughfare, the Sydney Bridge has a steel span 75 feet higher than the dome of Saint Pauls. The whole structure is 1650 feet long.

Continuing by rail we steamed up and up, right over the Blue Mountains, passing through most marvellous scenery. We then made a short stay at Brisbane where we arranged to meet Mr Curly Bell. In the course of a day or two he called on us.

I took to him at once. He was a fine young specimen of humanity, 26 years of age, a fine athlete, and of strong character. He said he was working on a big proposition that ought to appeal to both of us. He then unrolled some large coloured posters:-

B B B B B

5 B's

What do they mean?

[It was, in fact, an advertisement for *Bell's Bonza Buckjumping Broncos and Bullocks*. Curly Bell wanted Archie and Syd to join him as participants in his rodeo-type circus.]

Well, he took us along to his Homestead at Barralong where we stayed with him and his Aunt for a while. As my fellow emigrant, Captain Syd Whitaker, positively declined to do anything but as originally arranged, that is, farming, we decided to trek along together until we could fix up. Syd [being American] got a job quite soon but I went on and on meeting with no luck as far as farming was concerned. It struck me forcibly; that no English need apply?

[Reproduced here is a letter, written by Archie to an unknown friend, giving an account of his impressions of Australia, about five months after landing at Brisbane, whilst on his way to Longreach, Queensland.]

> My experiences here so far have not been quite so sweet or profitable as the The Organisers of the Officers Overseas Settlements Scheme had held out to us.
> After my four years in The Army and Flying Corps (now The Royal Air Force) I was to assist a farmer in the glorious sunshine of Australia. There they promised us a man's life - we should make much money - we should buy our own farm - settle down with a wife and family - and live happy ever afterwards. Yes a life and land fit for heroes! I fear, however, that The Organisers had been sadly misled.
> We discovered that 'Our Farmer' never had a Farm - a nice young gentleman indeed, a popular sportsman not much older than I. His name, Curly Bell. He had several branches to his Profession, the chief was keeping a gambling saloon and another was a buckjumping circus. After sampling both I decided to take up the latter branch which offered freedom, fresh air, and big money.
> Then for three months I was riding or being thrown from various animals, with great regularity.
> I next discovered that beyond good food, good company, and a few shillings, there was no other payment until we could stage a Show in one of the Towns.

This set me thinking and I expressed my ideas to Curley Bell for I did not wish to grow old in Longreach on his terms. I remember I was encouraged to smoke very long cigars as the Boss (Mr Curley Bell) said it gave an air of distinction to his Establishment.

I then decided to quit although the Boss was confident that we should make hundreds of pounds when we showed in Townsville.

"Well, my boy if you won't stop I'm sorry and I have no cash to settle up with you, for you have done good work. Take your favourite horse" - and in a further burst of generosity - "take these five good cigars. Smoke one whenever you go for a job; it makes you look the goods!"

Leaving Longreach I turned my horse towards Isis Downs. I was not too easy in my mind as to the future. I possessed a rough-riding kit, a service revolver and - 5 cigars. It hardly seemed a full equipment to make a fortune with, or even produce the next meal - unless I staged a hold-up. But there did not appear to be anything to hold-up in that part of Queensland. For many weeks I rode from one sheep station to another, without getting a job, but of course just temporary work.

I could however always rely on being given a good meal and a pleasant reception. They had no time for 'a pommy' on their farms! I was now getting thoroughly fed up with the endless plains, shimmering with heat and distorted with mirages: the jumping jacks, those balls of tangled grass which rolled and rolled along the plains at every puff of wind.

I was glad then to meet a lone rider on a fine horse. He gave me a curt greeting but gradually warmed up. Then he told me he was an owner jockey, who went round the towns following the race meetings, and putting it [his horse] in to the entries. As a rule he could pay his way, and also get a good bit of sport out of it. His name was Sam Perryman.

But now trouble had come along, he had had a bad fall injuring a leg and it was festering. He was going into the next town, where he had entered his horse for the races, and would consult a doctor about his injury. He suggested I should accompany him as I might get some sort of job there. So off we went together. The doctor who examined my chum's wound, said at once that it would be impossible for him to race that week. My friend became very moody and upset. He stated it was an important race meeting and it would be a serious thing for him, as he was sure of picking up quite a lot of money over it.

He asked if I would go in with him. "For," said he, "my horse can win some of those races on his own, all you have to do is stick on!"

"Right Oh," said I, "I am game."

I was to receive a generous percentage of the winnings. He warned me very seriously that bad feelings ran high whenever a stranger butted in, and as soon as they saw me, "I should be unpopular and in danger of a mishap."

Next day I had a trial run on the quiet. I thought I acquitted myself in fine style, but his sole comment was, "Lousy!"

Not in the least bit daunted I was determined to start in his 'entries'. The first was at the Blackall Summer Meeting. Next day, while I was in the town, several people spotted me and offered me drinks at the hotel.

I sensed that they wanted to find out something about my chances and I felt already that I was not wanted. Someone turned the eyes of the crowd on me by shouting out, "There is that damned pommy that brought that horse out with him! It won the Derby so I have heard."

Absurd as was this statement, the crowd appeared to believe it. At the earliest opportunity I moved off and went round to the hotel stables where the horses were put up, that is, The Prince of Wales Hotel. Leading the horse through the yard, I noticed a rough looking cripple with a crutch, pushing into me.

He started demanding some tobacco in a menacing manner, following it up by clutching my arm in no uncertain way. I tried to pull myself away when he slashed at my face with an arm that terminated in a steel hook, just missing my face. At the same time he screamed out, "Help! Attacking a poor cripple!"

The local people knew him to be a general nuisance and knew he could look after himself. I mounted and road off to my invalid friend (Sam Perryman) and acquainted him with my adventures. I got no sympathy from him.

"I told you so, perhaps you are lucky to have got away so cheap. You keep out of the town until I tell you!"

Next morning I cantered out to the creek hoping to get a shot at a duck or two, when I started to hear the whine of a bullet flying past me. Putting my spurs into the horse I beat it back to the Camp in record time. On that occasion I did not say anything about my experience.

That evening I was again riding around, when three toughs sprang at me out of a creek hole. One grabbed the bridle, another hung onto my leg and the third advised me in no uncertain terms that it would be the worse for me if I dared come into their race meeting.

"Let's chuck the damned pommy into the creek!" he bellowed to his confederates, "Perhaps that will teach him to remember what we say to him!"

He was in the act of unseating me, when I whipped out my revolver and let fly catching him in the knees, I should think. Anyway he rolled along the ground screaming and the other two rushed away in different directions disappearing into the bush like rabbits.

In fifteen minutes I was in the Chief Constable's office. when I got my breath I told him about my hold up, wanting to be first with my version. I said, "If that blackguard goes under don't blame me!"

He burst into laughter and clapped his hands with delight. "We hope you have killed at least one of them. We know the rogues, they are real scoundrels and will stop at nothing. They are the most difficult to get hold of. I expect they were paid to keep you out of the way. We have enough evidence to hang the lot twice over."

All these happenings made me think that I had dropped into a real serious business and not just a joy ride. I would keep out of "The Prince" that night. I would lie low until the Great Tomorrow!

Next day I repaired to the Blackall race Course with my chum, Sam Perryman. We had a good look round and saw the first race, unobserved by the section of spectators we were trying to avoid. The winner of the 1.30pm race was a bay mare, taken from a bakers cart. Much quarrelling and haggling took place with the Bookmakers at the settling.

My race debut was to be the 2.30pm race of 1 mile [1.6km]. I was all excitement when Sam piloted me to the starting gate. I concentrated on all the instructions he had hammered into me. My mount, *Flying Star*, was quoted at 5 to 1.

Away to an indifferent start, I lost ground but coming into the straight I ran into third place at the finish. I was conscious of things being thrown at me during the race but I was too engrossed on my job to bother then. Sam rushed around to pick up our 'place' money which came to a nice little sum.

My next race was at 4.30pm. The Blackall Sweepstakes of £50 over a distance of 9 furlongs. [1 furlong is 1/8 mile or 201 metres.] I had a feeling that I should do much this time. We decided to have a real plunge on our horse, especially at the useful price of 6 shillings. I was third favourite.

Away to a good start, I was in a good position, *Flying Star* setting the pace. With three hundred yards to go I burst right away from the field. Amid a volley of oaths, sticks and stones from the section of the crowd (which only goaded me to further effort) I passed the post an easy winner. Anyhow I was far too excited to know by how many lengths it happened to be.

Owing to the hostile attitude of a large mob, who were shouting, "No race!" Sam shoved me away and whispered, "Slip away through the fields and enter the back door of the Prince of Wales Hotel. Change and wait for me!"

Half an hour later Sam turned up with two friends and handed me my share of the stakes, as we had agreed together from the winnings. Very seriously he waved his fist at me saying, "Now then, you dark horse, you want to get to Barcaldine and Muttaborough - well, get along now and good luck to you. Don't stop for tea, go while the going is good!"

I laughed and replied, jokingly "Oh, all right, what's the hurry? I shall stop till tomorrow."

Sam became very excited and appealed to his two friends. "You had better have a word with this young fool."

"That's what we are," said one, flourishing a police certificate in my face. "We are guarding you, and if you don't slide away in fifteen minutes, Lord help you. There has been a lot of money dropped today and when the meeting breaks up there will be a rough house for someone."

Sam was at the door with my horse. We all shook hands and under their kind pressure I was up with my bundle and five miles beyond the Alice River before night fall. At the quiet home of a settler I had a good supper, and counted up the result of my first days racing.

I wrote to Mr Curley Bell at Muttaborough, as agreed, and he wired me to meet him at Sydney, IMMEDIATE AND URGENT!

5

LIFE IN AUSTRALIA

[This is a pen picture of life in a typical country town in the county of Mitchell, Queensland, drawn by Archie Filby while in Barcaldine, Queensland, in the summer of 1921.]

Barcaldine was en fete, as much as a town of its size could expect to be, although at the moment there was very little to indicate any difference from the ordinary run of days. The long main street was deserted. The only movement was from lazy clouds of yellow dust sweeping the lighter pieces of rubbish along with it to lodge them against the line of telephone poles which were all that divided the road from the footpath.

Inside the Shakespeare Hotel and the smaller bars things were more lively. This was the last day of the local races and, being the hour before lunch, the bars were packed with a crowd who were either anxious to get information regarding some horse or those who were only too anxious to give some.

Every few minutes a party would leave the bar carrying their glasses and would stand in the corner conferring in low tones, and another tip straight from the horse's mouth would be given. Actually most of the men there, and there were practically no women, were experienced horsemen, and could judge a horse fairly well. So that it was more the abilities of the jockeys that were discussed and not only their abilities, but whether they wanted to win the race in which they were running.

The crowd, although composed of men of all ages, fat men, lean men, tall or short, had a sameness about it which was typical of this part of Queensland. Mile after mile of the country showed the endless small bushes, some five or six inches in height, on which thousands of sheep seemed to thrive.

The few fences which ran for miles across the country seemed to hold the country together like a badly tied parcel, only emphasised the fact that one station differed very little from another. And now that the owners and hands had gathered together it seemed that the sameness extended to them.

Anyone wearing a complete suit was very much the exception. Most were dressed in an open-neck shirt, trousers pulled on over concertina riding boots, and a coat of some different colour. All in tones of brown or grey, faded by the strong sun and coated with dust.

Periodically they visited Longreach, as it was the end of the railway line, and from it wool and sheep were sent south. The sheep were packed tightly in double storied trucks so that they formed their own packing and would not be thrown from their feet by the jolting of the train.

Lately these long trains had crawled out of the station, almost as fast as they could be loaded, for the country was in the grip of a drought. Those station owners who could afford it were sending their sheep south to pasture. But it was an expensive business as a big percentage died on the way and the rolling stock of the railway was not large enough to cope with the demand.

From the corner of the long veranda that surrounded the Shakespeare Hotel came a roar of laughter as Max Morton gathered a jackpot. All the morning they had been playing and he had been losing steadily. Then a boy from his outlying station, 'Morton Downs', had ridden in with a note and, after which, he (Max) had become increasingly cheerful and with it his luck had become phenomenal.

Soon after the clatter of the dinner bell sounded the game broke up but Morton seemed to consider his luck at gambling worth pushing further. As the party made their way to the already crowded dining room he laid bets that there would be an odd number at their long table and that he would be the first to be served of their party. He also stated that his luck was so good that he was cancelling his last order for trucks and would send no more sheep south as he would take a gamble on it raining soon and saving most of them.

A neighbouring station holder, who was one of the party, offered a premium for the trucks which Morton wanted to cancel, refusing to even consider Morton's suggestion that he should also take a gamble on the rain coming within the next two weeks.

"If," he said to Morton, "you are so keen on a gamble, I'll sell you my entire flocks at what it would cost me to send them out, and bring them back, when the drought breaks. And I will offer to buy those that are still alive back, giving you a handsome profit if you can keep enough alive until the drought breaks. They can stop on my station and if all die I shall have been covered to a fair extent by your purchase price while if we get rain. And since you seem to be prepared to gamble on it, you will make a pretty decent sum."

Having calculated for a moment Morton roared, "I'll go you! You blokes are afraid to gamble on a certainty."

"Well," retorted the other, "if you are so keen on gambling, why didn't you enter your Mariana against my horse? As it is I'll give you three to one that nothing beats it this afternoon."

"I can get better odds than that from the bookies. But I'll bet you even money that I'll produce a horse from my stables that will beat yours."

"Done. Over what length?"

"From this telephone pole outside to the next one."

There had been a silence when the challenge was made. But now everyone started talking at once, for no Australian can resist a bet, especially an unusual one. Long odds were offered and accepted against Morton's horse, and when he announced that he was going to race the horse that his boy had ridden in on, there were roars of laughter. For although there were no bad horses in this part of the country, it certainly looked the worst.

A rangy looking animal of an indescribable roan colour, with abnormally long legs, and a fiddle-shaped head. Being old it had been turned out to find what food it could from around the station, and the diet of dried grass and dust had reduced it to a skeleton. That Morton was serious there could be little doubt as he had already wagered a large sum on his horse getting very long odds. But most of the onlookers thought it to be a joke against his neighbour.

The afternoons racing was over and again Morton's luck had been in and he had collected a handsome stake, most of it being made on the owner's horse that was to race his the following morning, it having run away with the field. During the evening Mortons taunts got stronger and stronger and by the end of the evening he was the owner of many thousands of sheep which, with no sign of the drought breaking, would certainly ruin him.

The next morning, heavy black shadows, made by the telegraph posts, crossed the main street of Barcaldine. The dark line cast by the one outside the Shakespeare Hotel made an excellent starting line for the novel race that was about to be run. A crowd lined both sides of the road waiting for the start.

It had been arranged that the horses should amble up to the line and that the start should be signalled by the beating of the large dinner gong belonging to the hotel. There had been some opposition to this but Morton had got his way and all was ready.

Morton's horse ambled out with the dejected air of one having to face the long amble back to the station. The other, with its coat shining in the morning sunlight, reared and pranced and scattered the near-by crowd. At last he was induced to face the right way and move towards the starting line.

Bang went the gong and with one convulsive effort Morton's horse leapt for safety down the street. A few more erratic jumps and it was past the second post and heading for home in a series of pitching jumps. The race horse had sprung sideways, away from the noise, and had then picked up its running. It now passed Morton's horse with ease and then circled back again. But those first bounds had covered the distance to the next post before it had got into its stride.

The losers considered they had been tricked but rather appreciated the joke was on them especially when Morton admitted that the horse had been badly frightened many times by the station gong when it was being broken in and had unseated the rider by its terrific leaps.

The Barcaldine fete was over; the clank of trucks running over the points was again in full swing. Sheep baaed and raised clouds of dust as they were driven into the loading pens, while the station owners and hands hastily saddled up and set off into the heat haze. Late that evening Morton arrived home.

As he approached the well-built homestead, the sounds of a military band came to his ears and a satisfied smile appeared on his face. Calling a boy to take his mount he went inside to be met by his wife and daughter, whose first question was, "Did you get the note?"

"Yes. You're sure you got the news right?"

"Absolutely, it has never come over so clearly as it did yesterday while the news tonight confirmed it and said that the rains were spreading inland from Bowen to the coast!"

"Well, I have bought what seems nearly all the sheep left in the district but I suppose I shall have to let most of them off with a small payment. But I don't think we shall be laughed at again for the purchase of what they called 'the new fangled wireless!'"

The story of my Australian travels is resumed on the next page.

6

AN ILL-FATED EXPEDITION THROUGH THE WILDS OF SOUTH-WEST AUSTRALIA.

While journeying on horseback from Port Augusta to Lake Everard, South Australia, I was persuaded to undertake the job of tracing an Explorer named Leichardt who had gone to Coolgadie Gold Mines and never been heard of since.

[Friedrich Wilhelm Ludwig Leichardt was a German explorer and naturalist, most famous for his exploration of northern and central Australia. He successfully completed, in 1845, a 4,800 kilometre (3,000 mile) expedition between the Darling Downs in Queensland and Port Essington in the Northern Territory. In 1848, he set off on another expedition, from the Condamine River in Queensland, and headed for the Swan River in Perth. He, and all the members of his expedition, were never heard from again. Although several expeditions were dispatched to find him, very little was found to explain what had happened to Leichardt or the other members of the expedition.]

My outfit was a wagon and 14 horses replete with provisions, tools and maps. My only companion was a native named Jake, a hefty fellow well fitted for months of trekking. I calculated on a 1,200 mile trek and a large share of luck. Our send off was a solemn and funereal business or so it seemed to me as the cortège, I mean 'outfit', got into its stride.

I became unpleasantly impressed with my companion and as time rolled on he became sullen and tongue tied. I preferred my horses to his company and had figured out a plan to dump him on the first party I came across.

My itinerary was away out into The Black Blocks or Never-Never Lands through the Nullabor Plains and waterless Deserts towards Coolgardie. By now I had taken to sleeping with one eye on Jake - I did not like him! We had covered about 700 miles [1126 km] and were now on the Plains of Nullabor, an endless desert of sand, scrub and desolation and, of course, waterless.

It was there I had a real shock and a narrow shave for my life. I was cooking breakfast and prodding the eggs and bacon with a large skewer, when my eye chanced to roam to my shaving mirror on the ground. In a flash I saw a black box coming down from the sky behind me. I sprang aside and discovered Jake bringing down a large cooking pot in an attempt to brain me. I slashed the frying pan in his face and followed up with my skewer then planted my boot in his stomach as he came for me.

Yes, he was a hefty chap indeed and a struggle for life went on until I got astride of him and beat him senseless before I fell away utterly exhausted. Next I roped him up and dragged him into the waggon before he came to. By that time he was securely chained as well. It was a terrible position: miles from civilisation with a team of 14 horses and a madman to look after as well as myself.

Over a good breakfast (for one) and a cigar I decided to continue West and perhaps reach Kalgoorlie, I might do it in two or three days if lucky. I would dump all my heavy baggage and shoot 6 of the horses rather than abandon them to their fate. This I did and my funereal train moved on. That night I dozed with a chain on my wrist and attached to Jake's leg to warn me of any movement.

He did not recognise me and his ravings disturbed my rest. Before sunrise I was about working when I heard some queer noises coming across the desert. Then through my glasses I figured it was a mob of wild cattle or maybe a caravan of mostly camel or quite possibly a bandit gang. They had been very busy lately I had been warned. I immediately galloped barebacked to intercept them. I must have help at once!

My luck was in: it was a large camel caravan going east with such valuables as wines, gold, lead and fine woods. They listened to my explanation in wonder telling me I was a young fool to attempt the journey with one man. They at once gave me every assistance.

They told me it was quite a common occurrence to find men in Jake's condition, scores of men had gone raving mad in those pitiless regions and it was doubtful if we got him back alive. I had had more than enough of my expedition and I decided to join the caravan.

With Jake securely locked in the waggon, I at length made good the return journey of my ill-fated expedition.

7

TALLY HO! THE TALLYMAN. A NARROW SQUEAK.

Syd Whitaker and I then tried our luck in the Tallyman business. We heard there was a constant demand for suits, underclothes, and various odds and ends by the workers in isolated districts and mining villages throughout Queensland. Big profits could be easily made.

We put a considerable amount of money into the venture and off we went. We travelled by mules, the only method of transport in some places. Two of these fine animals were packed high with goods, and we rode one more each carrying our personal outfit and provisions. Trade was good and between times we thoroughly enjoyed ourselves and got plenty of good sport.

After a while the rainy season started and the continual deluge put an abrupt end to our travels. The country became waterlogged and each river we swam or forded became more difficult and dangerous.

Finally, in swimming the swollen Burdekin River, all our stores and stocks were swept away, together with the four mules. After repeated and desperate efforts I retrieved our cash bag, then with great difficulty we reached a small settlement and weighed up our unfortunate position.

Well, we agreed we might have been worse off - for not only had I nearly lost my life in that swirling torrent - I was all but beaten and drowned, trying to save at least one floundering mule! It was touch and go! It certainly was a very narrow squeak!

We tramped on next day and put up in the town of Ingham. Whitty had already cabled to his girl, Steve, in England to come out to him, and soon after she joined us in the business.

I decided, however, to dissolve the partnership with them and strike out for the Prairie and Pampas Lands. Motoring through Ingham a year later, I found the firm of Whitaker still there, but they were contemplating a very early return to London.

8

THE TAMING OF A TARTAR

When I first saw Jim Reed he was operating a gambling game in Barcaldine: one of the smaller towns in central Queensland and almost the last place on the railway line, it consisted merely of a double row of tin-roof houses lining a dusty street.

My visit happened to coincide with with one of the small local fairs, and the place was full of a motley crowd of sheep herders and station holders from the surrounding country, wool buyers, shearers, jockeys, and the inevitable racing touts and card sharpers.

Strolling aimlessly round the town with a chap I had met at the hotel, the foreman of a sheep-shearing gang, an occupation which would have seemed unduly rough and hazardous to a blue-nosed sea skipper of the old type, my attention was attracted to a knot of people standing in the light of an acetylene flare.

"What's going on there?" I asked.

"Jim Reed's game most likely; want to see it?"

"Is it likely to be interesting?"

"I should think so; Reed's reckoned to be one of the toughest men in this part of the world."

This, coming from my friend, was a surprising remark, for he himself was just about the toughest individual you could meet in a day's march. So we edged our way through the crowd that pressed round a light rail enclosing a table on one end of which was spread a cloth divided into three sections, one red, one white and one blue.

In the centre of the table stood a shallow tin receptacle, which had again been divided into compartments, an equal number painted in each of the three colours. When the customers had placed their stakes on the cloth, a ball was thrown into the tin, where it bounced wildly for a few moments from one compartment to another before coming to rest, when odds would be paid to those who had backed the winning colour.

The far end of the table was occupied by an imposing pile of notes and silver, on top of which lay a revolver, and as we approached I heard the man who was running the game remark, in an incongruously quiet and peaceful tone, "Anyone who likes can rob this lot, and he'll probably get away with it. But I'll get him later."

I looked at the man with considerable interest. Certainly there was nothing in his appearance to suggest that he was a person held in awe. His clothing was nondescript, he gave no hint of great muscular strength, and indeed the fine fair hair blowing this way and that on his forehead made him look almost effeminate.

He operated his game in a rather apologetic manner, raking in the handsome profits which came to him with each throw of the ball with an air of distaste, as though he really preferred paying out.

A few days later I was making the short railway journey from Barcaldine to Aramac and was about to board the train when I saw him entering another compartment. My curiosity having been thoroughly aroused by the tales I heard of him, I deliberately followed him into his carriage and sat down beside him.

Conversation started naturally soon after the train pulled out, and he told me that he was doing well with his gambling table but that the police were getting more and more troublesome and indirect bribes were becoming increasingly heavy.

"It's an easy enough life, though," he said, "and I travel pretty light, as you can see. All my outfit goes comfortably on the luggage rack."

As he spoke, his gaze travelled upward to the rack above our heads, empty but for my bag, then shot across to the rack on the other side, which was entirely vacant. When he saw that his stuff had not been put on the train, an amazing transformation came over his face. Its lines seemed to fade out like an over-touched photograph, while the eyes took on a peculiar opaque appearance.

From lips that hardly moved he emitted a string of the foulest imaginable oaths, and in the slow movement of a sleepwalker he drew a large Swedish clasp-knife from his pocket and snapped the blade into place with a loud click. He seemed oblivious of my presence, and I sat watching him in fascination but ready to spring up at once if necessary.

His back was towards me now, however, and I might as well not have been there for all the notice he took of me. He bent forward and with measured precision slit the cushion on the opposite seat from end to end. Then, with the first quick gesture he had made with the discovery of his loss, he flicked the knife out of the window and stood staring expressionlessly at the passing bush until we rolled into the dusty little station of Aramac.

The town didn't offer much choice of accommodation, so not unnaturally Jim Reed and I came face to face in the bar of the one hotel. He apologised for his behaviour on the train, but in a perfunctory manner, as one might apologise for knocking against somebody in a crowd, then launched into a series of interesting tales of his travels in the back blocks of Queensland.

When he had left the bar I heard, from various bystanders, more stories in which he figured largely. Some swore that he was a maniac, while others were emphatic that he was perfectly sane, but all dwelt on his cold rages, his cruelty, his Herculean strength, and above everything, his complete absence of fear. It was, they said, not the courage of a brave man in the ordinary sense, but a man who had no idea what it was to be afraid.

Of his cruelty I soon had evidence, for the next evening he was standing at the bar, alone as usual, when his drink was knocked over by a skylarking boundary rider. I saw that extraordinary change come over his face, and with a movement so neat that he hardly seemed to move at all, he laid the man out, then as his adversary lay on the floor, he deliberately ripped the heel of his heavy boot along his upturned face.

Although the place was full, no-one stirred until he had again turned towards the bar and ordered another drink.

The following morning I left for Longreach, and to my profound astonishment he came to the station to see me off. He appeared to have taken a peculiar fancy to me, perhaps because, like himself, I was an Englishman. I noticed that his face was badly cut about and bruised, but he made no comment and I didn't ask questions. One of my travelling companions, however, told me that friends of the man whom he had knocked out in the bar had waylaid him.

"Two of 'em are in hospital," he added.

For three months I was travelling in the North, but at Hughenden, Townsville, and even as far away as Ingham, stories were told of this lonely, untamed man. It seemed that now and then he threw up his gambling and went for long stretches into the bush, accompanied only by one native boy. On one of his excursions he had attempted to follow up Landsborough's tracks.

[William Landsborough (1825-1886) was an explorer and surveyor and headed the first expedition to cross Australia from north to south.]

Doubting that this pioneer surveyor had, as most people thought, been killed by the Blacks, he rather favoured the theory that he had got lost and run out of water, a fate that Reed himself had nearly shared, for his horses had died and he had carried his boy for several miles, eventually bringing him to the railway line.

[Archie is mistaken in suggesting that Landsborough had 'been killed by the Blacks'. Perhaps he was confusing him with Leichardt.]

There he had stopped a train, and having put his boy on board and paid for him to receive attention - an act of mercy strangely at variance with what I knew of his ruthless nature - he had filled his water bottles and gone off into the bush once more, only to turn up at some small town or other more taciturn than ever.

And then I met him again, in Blackall. He was buying uncut stones from diggers in the sapphire fields, which were making much of him, and he seemed in his cold, detached way to be friendly with a rangy-looking station holder and his wife, a pretty, dark-eyed Jewess.

I was introduced, and the girl, whom he addressed as Lily,

recounted breathlessly the story of how Bill, her husband, visiting an itinerant buck-jumping show, had accepted a challenge to ride a bucking bullock. The circling [rope] round the bullock's body, to which Bill had held when riding, had broken and the bullock had first thrown its rider and then gored him.

But before any serious injury had been done, Jim Reed had leapt over the wall of the stockade, seized the animal's long, widespread horns in either hand, and with this leverage and his terrific strength, forced it over on its side and held it down until help was forthcoming.

It was clear that the girl was far gone in hero-worship, but it was impossible for me to judge from Reed's impassive manner to what extent her admiration was reciprocated.

Presently all three left the bar together, and when I went there the next day I found an excited group of men energetically talking among themselves. Catching the name Reed I strolled up to them and enquired what had happened.

Somewhat to my surprise, I learned that late the previous night, Lily had decided to elope with her hero, and her husband's protests had merely caused Reed to fling him bodily through a glass window. The pair had taken the early morning train out of town, leaving the husband in a critical condition.

It must have been about a year later that, travelling on the ferry, which runs across Sydney Harbour carrying people from the city to the residential suburbs, I noticed something disturbingly familiar in the profile of a man near me.

He was a typical business man, in a well-cut blue lounge suit, with a neat bowler hat, and carrying under his arm a leather brief-case. Puzzled, I stared at him for a few moments, then as he turned his head I saw him full-face. I went over and touched him on the arm.

"Hullo, Reed," I said.

He seemed pleased enough to see me, but his whole bearing had subtly changed. There was a suggestion almost of nervousness in his manner. I asked him what he was doing with himself, and he told me he had a job in an insurance office, and was now hurrying home to his wife. To my suggestion that he should have a drink with me when we got ashore, he replied quietly, "No, thanks, old man, don't touch it these days. Lily doesn't approve."

This was something of a shock, and as I pondered on the astonishing change time and matrimony had wrought in the man, someone on the ferry cried out and pointed excitedly. I looked up to see a huge waterspout, not altogether an uncommon sight in those parts, whirling towards the Heads, the two great cliffs that form the entrance to the bay.

I turned to speak to Reed, but was instantly silenced by his expression. He was watching the towering column of spinning water, and the look in his eyes was unmistakable - it was a look of abject terror.

This was the last time I ever saw Jim Reed. But I prefer to remember him as he was before he was tamed.

9

BELL'S BONZA BUCKJUMPING BRONCOS AND BULLOCKS

Curley Bell expounded a big scheme which, he said, "Would suit us if we would come in."

Well, Curley had a persuasive way with him and we jumped to it.

"It will be a grand success," said he. Failure was not in his lexicon.

"I am producing a Wild West Show that will startle the natives," he continued, "I know what the Aussies like."

We spent much time and money advertising, scouring the State of Queensland for trick shooters, stock-whip experts, professional bronco busters and all that sort of thing.

We acquired over 50 selected horses, donkeys, bullocks, ponies, and set to work in earnest practicing the manifold parts. Curley appeared to be a born cowboy and showed us all the tricks of the trade in shooting and riding. We all made good headway.

The Woolloongabba Cricket Ground was leased and we attired ourselves in bright red shirts, yellow breeches, wide leaf hats, concertina leggings, elastic riding side-boots, and large silver spurs. Also elaborate trappings and harnesses for the horses and a holster containing a 32 automatic revolver.

The professionals were curious chaps but quite decent: there was Snowie Coogan, Con Macaulay, Jock Carver, the latter was also a stock-whip expert. They 'guyed' me as a new chum. They kidded me to get across some of the buckjumpers. I had a go at several of the animals but was thrown with great regularity.

When I had got used to the creatures coming at me with open mouths and frisking playfully around trying to pat me on the head with their hoofs, plus other little pranks, I was allowed to join in the processions through the towns.

We had a bit of excitement on one occasion. We each rode an animal of some sort and led out the worst of the rogues and buckjumpers, such as Centipede, Black Bess, Getaway, Aeroplane, Prince and Whipcord. Also a bullock and donkey or two.

Curley was leading the parade cracking his whip playfully at the sightseers and holding forth to the population of Brisbane about, "The Finest Show on Earth. Bronco Busting, Wild Bull Riding, Unique Exhibitions of Horsemanship. Who wants £5 a minute? Come on you little boys. Free Donkey Rides and 10 shillings to take your gal out with. Great Silver Cups given away. Only a few seats left. Hurry up! Hurry up for the tickets!"

We all assisted by giving forth war whoops and Coo-ees and behaving like lunatics to the great amusement of the throng, when one of the horses broke away. That was a signal for a general stampede.

Away they raced, across Victoria Bridge and down George Street. Curley went tearing after the mob, shouting orders, the crowd screaming and racing for their lives. Eventually we rounded up most of them in a paddock and got our breath back again.

Then up came a posse of Police armed with note books, enquiring for the manager to issue summonses and assessing the damages. Curley Bell took the officers into a private room at a nearby Hotel to give full particulars. Things were looking very serious for us and also some of the citizens and their wives were becoming threatening.

I took up a position as door keeper and I noticed, as I kept my foot in the door, that bottles and glasses appeared from nowhere. The stern voices seemed to turn to banter, then roars of laughter, as Curley reeled off some of his backwood yarns. Then there was a clicking of heels and out marched the Police in good spirits: each with a circus ticket for himself and his family. So the day was saved.

I now did some practicing on the sly. The only riding I had done before I left home was on other people's animals that were turned out to graze in the meadows. Really that was pretty good training and quite helpful. They had no harnesses and they usually careered through woods, rivers, and fences until they fell or I was thrown off. Now I tried work with the lasso, had a go with the stock-whip and practiced more riding.

Great was their surprise one day when I was told to "Lasso that bullock and look lively". I promptly brought him down only to be chased for my life next minute: I quickly scaled a ten foot fence.

The great day came when Bell's Bonza Buckjumping Broncos and Bullocks Show opened at the 'Gabba Cricket Ground. We were all excitement. The tickets for seats sold like hot cakes. The weather was very wet and humid. We were up at half past four in the morning. We turned our hands to this, that and the other, supplementing our work with continuous chatter and bantering one another in proper Australian style.

The great hour struck for the wonderful 'circus' to begin. Attired in my glorious scarlet shirt and yellow breeches, I took my cue from the band and plunged into the arena on my beautiful but tricky mare, Black Bess. Bare backed and with only a bridle we went full gallop round the Ring accompanied by the cracking of the stock-whip of Curly Bell, the Ringmaster, to the excited yells of the audience.

With rifle shots I then riddled eggs, hats, boots and other articles that were thrown in the air while the mare kept up her mad gallop. Anyway, our performance was rewarded with much applause. The horsemanship of the professionals was the finest I have ever seen.

Then there was the trick of flicking a lighted cigarette out of the lips of a young woman by means of a forty foot stock-whip welded by Jock Carver. That and many other turns kept the crowd, including myself, well-entertained.

At nine o'clock, to the accompaniment of bells, trumpets and drums, my extra special turn was announced:

"Slim Phill will ride any unbroken mustang or bullock anyone can bring into the ring, saddled, for one minute. The wager will be £5 a side, cash down!"

Three foot coloured posters had been stuck all round the Towns showing Slim Phill. (I certainly was slim in build in those days.)

[Archie was called 'Phill' because of his surname, Filby.]

Now I strode into the arena and held up my hand for (comparative) silence and planked down my £5 carefully selected from a very heavy ponderous leather purse of 'Cash'. I slammed down each golden sovereign on the little table, ringing them noisily, while the Ringmaster introduced me and repeated the conditions:

"This young backwoodsman will ride any kind of animal you bring into the ring, for one full minute. Wager £5 a side. Come along chums, come along. Five pounds a minute all for nothing!"

The first horse and man to appear I did not quite like the look of. Both were quiet and sullen. Which was the greatest rogue, man or animal, I could not fathom. When the money was down, Curley Bell sauntered across to the pair, ran his hands over the snorting animal, and said, "Ah! That's better my friend," and he appeared to put something in his pocket.

"Come along now," yelled Curley, "it's Slim Phill's special turn. You all know the conditions, Poley Saddle, Flank Rope, Spurs Only."

He rubbed his chin with his clenched fist as he looked menacingly at the owner of the horse. I suppose I was lucky, for I stuck on that wild buckjumper for the specified time of 60 seconds, but it seemed more like 60 minutes to me.

Then Curley wheeled on the man and growled, "Get out quick or I will show the crowd these," and he produced some razor edged thorns from his pocket. "They will skin you if they do get hold of you!" It was not altogether a new trick to put needles under the crupper to send an animal mad with pain.

Several Old Sports and Cowpunchers dragged or shoved their weird looking animals through the entrance in the hopes of picking up an easy fiver. I was excused from trying out a ferocious young bull, as they were quite unable to saddle it. I apologised to the audience and told them I was more disappointed than they were, but hoped it would be saddled in time for tomorrow's display, when I would show them something that would astonish them.

I usually made a rush and threw myself across an animal as soon as it appeared, which gave me the advantage of the hands that were helping for the moment. The cunning owners, usually real toughs, stood around to collect the dough off me. I was gaining much valuable experience and was showing a good profit on the day's work.

I began to feel that I should now be alright for the Grand Finals to be run off in a Three Days Contest at Easter, March 17th, 18th and 19th. It was open to all comers. Valuable cups would be given. Alas and alack a serious drama occurred, and I was the tragedian!

It was in a mass display of horsemanship and I was hanging on to one of our stud, a wild Arab type of mustang named Silver. Suddenly it bolted out and jumped between some posts which fell towards us, catching my left leg and pitchforking me into the air, landing me in a heap. I was quite unable to move so I lit a cigar.

Curley, Bob and a crowd of onlookers came to my rescue. I had a beastly wound extending from my knee to half way up my side. By the time they had treated it with boiling water and iodine, the ambulance had arrived. I think the hospital patients forgot all about their pains when they saw 'Slim Phill' from Bell's Buckjumpers brought in, in full war paint. The Press that night came out with big placards and headlines:

THE TERRIBLE ACCIDENT AT THE 'GABBA CIRCUS.

There *were* 5 Big Bs, you may remember, but I produced a sixth one bigger than the lot. [I'm not sure what Archie meant by this. I can only guess...]

In spite of the Aussies' great kindnesses I got fed up at the inaction and at the end of two weeks I wrote to Curley asking him to bring along some civilised clothes so I could escape on sticks. This was done and I joined my old friends of the 5 B's once again. After the Easter Show we repeated in Toowoomba and Ipswich.

Although my leg and side were very tender, I could not miss the fun. I rode the old buckjumper, Getaway, (now fairly broken) and we took to the road again. We drove the whole outfit along - 20 awkward horses, 10 bullocks, and 10 donkeys. 'Ginger' was hot-stuff, and she doubled back to Woolloongabba, chased by Bob and Snowie. That left me with the lot.

Some would gallop ahead, some wander into the bush while others would not move at all. As I could not get out of the saddle with any chance of getting back again, I engaged a useful lad. That night we all got together again, and we rounded up the lot in a yard. Off again at daybreak, Snowie riding Silver, Bob riding Rickety Kate. But my Getaway had smashed chicken runs and fences before they had captured her for me.

We continued our tour with the outfit through Queensland villages. It seemed to pour with rain day and night, and what with one thing and another, such as long working hours, snatched meals, and the legacy left me from my accident, my health became seriously affected.

One evening we reached the Fair Ground of Toowoomba with our circus. Our Managing Director, Curley Bell, had gone on in advance to fix up good quarters for man and beast. I spotted him immediately as he moved about giving instructions and giving a helping hand to all. (Curley never asked a man to do a thing he was unable to do himself.)

I rode over to him with a hearty, "How do you do?"

For answer he wheeled round on me and bellowed, almost in a rage, "What game are you having? A nice mess you are in!" Then quietly, "now my young Phill, keep on that horse and go straight along to Mrs Laisters Boarding House down Main Street and go to bed till I fetch you. You look like a damned ghost on strike."

Well, I readily agreed as I was unable to stand or help much. My bad leg and the shaking up had left me queer, while the arduous days of travelling and cow punching had taken a big toll on my strength. My surgeon gravely warned me I was to obey his advice if I valued my left leg.

A comfortable bed, good feeds, hot baths and nursing was excellent physic and I soon made headway. At the end of about ten days our Full Dress Buckjumping and Horsemanship Show was due to open up at the Toowoomba Fair Ground. I was sufficiently recovered to be able to do something to assist.

Anyway I was most anxious not to miss the auspicious occasion. Under pressure they offered me some light duties in the Booking and

Ticket Offices. I was put in charge of the ticket sellers, marshalling the jostling crowds, warning the free gate-crashers, and firmly but effectively dealing with the "drunks and undesirables".

I found that my *light* duties were very heavy and exacting. I envied my chums decked up in their finery, mounted on a thoroughbred, proudly showing off its paces to an admiring audience. I was determined to report myself as A-1 Copper Bottom next time.

That day business was good. Between times I cast my eye on the Circus Show inside. I had heard so much from the professionals, while I recuperated, about their wonderful turns, delivered to me in their best bedside tones. I had said in reply "Oh yeah?" thinking they were boasting and leg-pulling. Now I saw they were telling the truth and I was highly entertained.

It was certainly great fun and the whole show was a great credit to Curley Bell who had unearthed so many good and skilful turns and reproduced them. He was certainly a born showman and organiser. He could get a kick out of a thing that cost nothing and it would go down as well or better than a star turn that cost fifty guineas a week.

A wonderful trapeze act or lion performance often failed to create the sensation or attention in proportion to the huge expenditure. Some patrons might just close their eyes with boredom but did anyone sleep when the donkey race for boys was on?

10

THE DONKEY RACE FOR BOYS

The whole audience rocked and roared with laughter at the antics which were so skilfully produced in this wholesome event. It was a proper put-up job: a joke on the boys, this Donkey Race!

The bugles sounded a fan-fare. Curley Bell stands dramatically aloft on a big tub, in his gay outfit. He is superman. Mentally and muscularly, a fine looking man. He puts up the megaphone and booms forth, "Any little boy like a little ride on a little donkey? Ten Bob for riding just once round the Ring for the winner! They are nearly too old to stand. So whack 'em up! Nothing to pay! Gold prizes for nothing! Now, boys, tumble up!

The ring becomes black with clamouring youngsters. Curley marshals them up with his whip handle amid much amusement and jollity. He yells, "Order! Order!" above the din. He seizes lads with hairy growths upon them, and says, "You Grandpapas can buzz off!" A lot of saucy girls he gently leads away by the hair, telling them, "Your mother is calling you!"

Holding up a hand for attention, Curley shouts, "I am going to have a lung test for qualification. Now listen! When I count THREE you must say: BELLS, BONZA, BUCKJUMPING, BRONCOS AND BULLOCKS! And let me hear you. One, two, THREE!"

How those kids yelled. After each test a bunch were weeded out until the surplus was eliminated. Now this was a cute wheeze of Curley's, killing two birds with one stone. The terrible yells of 'Bells, Bonza, Buckjumping, Broncos and Bullocks' was carried on the air right through the Town and beyond. Surely a *sound* advertisement?

At long last they line up. Crack goes the starter's pistol. Ten donkeys and ten hefty boys on their backs whacking into them. Two donkeys lie down! Two go the opposite way! Others go in circles or stand like a rock. But look! There they go amid much excitement! Two of the runners are within 30 yards of the Winning Post, going like Derby winners, their jockeys throwing sneering remarks at the also rans.

"Once around the Ring!" Curley bawls encouragingly, "stick in your knees! Ten bob first, five bob second!" [A 'bob' is slang for a shilling.]

It's all over. NO! Others are coming up. Only a few yards now. A big feed trough is spied by the hungry donkeys. They rush across to investigate, nearly capsizing it in their haste. Down go their noses, over their heads go their riders into the feed box, legs waving out of the luscious hay. Crack! Crack! Crack! goes the Ringmaster's stockwhip like an explosion and the startled donkeys canter past the winning post - riderless.

So the merry days went on. After showing in the principal Towns in Queensland and Victoria, our various contracts expired and the jolly old circus party dispersed at Ipswich after a farewell dinner. With heartfelt farewells we promised to meet again, perchance our good friend Curley Bell would put up another travelling show? It had been a glorious adventure: interesting work, considerable profit, and above all a man's life.

I took the addresses from Curley, Len and Bob. We promised that if the occasion arose for further adventure or business we would fix up together again and so on.

I took a rest, for a few weeks. I sent a letter to Captain Syd Whitaker, my original voyage chum, who I came 'out' with. He had pressed me to join him away up in Ingham, a rather primitive sort of a Town up in the hills, the usual transport seemed to be by mule.

My next move, however, was a long trek from Ipswich, right away through Queensland, by horseback, train and boat. Young Leonard Franklin, a chum from our show, was with me: a well-read and interesting partner. We visited scores of notable places.

We were carried away by the beauty of the magnificent country and the grandeur of the rugged mountains. I could fill a volume with the many wonderful and interesting things we encountered on that trip. During our peregrinations we called upon Curley Bell and also Syd Whitaker, both were fine. We again undertook to fix up something in the near future.

Len and I, after leaving the circus at Ipswich, made our way to Rockhampton, and joined in the big Carnival. I was greatly interested in the Cattle Drafting and Branding Competition. Continuing through Barcaldine, Aramac, and Longreach we took a train to Winton, then Hughenden. Leaving the line we obtained horses and rode across to Richmond and Camelford, the edge of beyond. They say if you once cross you stay there for seven years; and many curious cases were quoted.

We stayed a week at the pretty little suburb of Townsville. There the oranges, lemons, bananas, coconuts and mangos grow wild in great profusion. On again to the mining district of Ingham where all goods are conveyed by mule pack. We made rafts of bamboo poles, sailing the lakes and having plenty of diving and swimming.

A visit to the mines was made. The population was chiefly yellow and black, but we found the Europeans were a good class crowd and they gave us a good time. We also inspected the Victoria Sugar Refinery, quite an exhibition. [This refinery is near Ingham in the Shire of Hinchinbrook, Queensland.]

At Halifax our hotel proprietor suggested we should go in the garden and see his little pets. They consisted of a dozen crocodiles, twenty snakes and other charming creatures. That evening we went crocodile shooting. What a row they make, barking like wolves and braying like asses. I came across a huge snake, it appeared a foot round, so I gave it a wide berth as I detest all kinds of reptiles excessively.

Innisfail was our next call. It has the unenviable distinction of ranking amongst the highest rainfalls in the world. It was in that district that I nearly lost my life in the floods when they took our barren mules and all our worldly goods. Once more at Townsville to pick up Len then on to Blackall to join Curley and Whitty. Curley and myself made a trip to Charleville via Tambo and Augathella.

We ran into a cyclone, that was all but 300 yards [275 metres] away. The centre of the cone was travelling along, whirling everything into the air, leaving a clear road through the bush. We got some good shooting. We struck a flight of ducks and turkeys also a sounder of swine, so our larder was well stocked. Next day we obtained two emus and a kangaroo. On all these trips we greatly preferred to live, eat and sleep in the open, obtaining our own tucker and cooking.

11

TREKKING

It was October 1921 when I reached Aramac in Queensland. I sent off a telegram to Curley Bell at Longreach as arranged. In a day or so I received a reply from Curley asking me to join him and his Circus Troupe at Townsville as soon as convenient.

Having made the acquaintance of a young fellow named Tom Tighe, who like myself was trekking 250 miles [400 km] south, we got together some sort of an outfit. The chief things were 2 good saddle horses, 2 good dogs, fishing tackle, a 303 and a 32/40 gun and two 0.3 automatics. Also shot guns, ammunition, cutlery, and a small quantity of provisions. And off we started for Prairie.

Late that night we made our first camp by a dam on the Johnson River not far from Winton. With thoughts of the larder I stalked around and bagged a brace of ducks which we quickly cooked and enjoyed for supper.

At daybreak we pushed on again before the heat of the day and after several rests we finally made Ten Mile Bore. We had a shot at some large turkeys but they were much too wild to get hold of and we contented ourselves with small game.

That night we welcomed a Teamster with he long team of 16 horses yoked to a waggon-load of 10 tons of wool. he proved to be an interesting old boy and I well remember the songs and yarns we had round the camp fire. [These are related in the next chapter.]

At daybreak we were on our way again, although we lost some valuable breath and time catching our elusive horses. I made a detour to try and get some sugar.

We made camp at Nine Mile Bore that evening. It was just a shaft sunk, with rough casing to shore it up. The force of the water created quite a young fountain which made it extra inviting both for ourselves and our animals. I had shot at some of the animals and birds which hovered around the spring, obtaining some tern and duck, on which we made a sumptuous repast.

Our next camp was made at Muttaburra, a typical old Queensland town. The mail coach came thundering in with its six horses amid much noise. Horses were changed as well as parcels and news. A motley crowd of drovers, teamsters, farmers, hunters and cowpunchers vied with each other in shouting and showing off themselves, their horses and their dogs. A mixed market was being held close by. I have never seen such a miscellaneous collection of animals and goods offered for sale or barter.

While I was taking a little refreshment in the doorway of a shack, the porch darkened by the capacious form of a farmer with a bull on a halter. The bull's head was too big to enter without first tipping its head sideways, and as I did not like its hot breath or bloodshot eyes, I politely passed the beer jug out to the farmer. I thought there was nothing lost in being polite, especially as there was no emergency exit from the shack.

Tom was not for stopping in the town of Muttaburra, as it meant more cash than we wished to spend just then, so we continued our trek towards Prairie. We took with us a good supply of provisions such as tea, sugar, treacle, jam, fish, flour, mutton chops and tobacco. Following the banks of the Johnson River we branched off at the junction of the Landsborough River and made camp. We soon got a good fire going, the billy-pot boiling, and chops cooking in our up-to-date camp oven. All was well.

A little later on the dogs turned out a half-grown wild pig, just across the river. We rushed down with our guns and after a while I brought him down with a good shot under the ear. Tom and I swam across with visions of roast pork for supper. We found, though, that the porker was too heavy to tow across.

We were greatly startled by a commotion and on looking up the river bank we saw a large old boar towering above us. He was swinging his enormous head from side to side. Stamping and grunting at us, his terrible eyes and filthy mouth altogether made a most unpleasant picture. He was a ferocious brute with tusks a foot long. This incident was more than we had bargained for. We had only our knives with us and we were in real danger.

"What could we do about it?" we hurriedly asked each other as we backed away from His Lordship.

We dared not run. We knew quite well that he would delight in running us down and goring us. One can always back the boar. They are terribly fierce and cunning, when on the war path, as many a poor fellow can testify who has taken part in 'pig sticking'.

The dogs now took the matter in hand without any urging from us. A fight to the death seemed likely, judging by the awful din and the deadly rushes of the animals. The boar rushed from one to the other with murderous intent. After trampling one of the dogs to earth he plunged his way into the bush, much to our great relief. We hastily cut off the hind quarters of our porker, then made a small raft and towed it across the river.

We now set to work cutting the pork into joints, roasting some, baking and boiling the rest. The fat was rendered down and put into kerosene tins for future attention. Oh what a glorious supper we had of roast pork and vegetables!

As it was still quite light we thought we would take the opportunity of doing an hour's fishing. Not forgetting the alarm we had had, this time we took our guns with us. We soon got some bites and landed a number of good size yellow-bellied salmon and black bream.

As we were both very tired and sleepy we returned to our camp and made a big fire with piles of wood and turf. To keep away insects, pigs, and lots of other roaming animals, we placed netting all round and turned in for the night after a most successful day.

We thought next day was Sunday so we rested and put our outfit in order. Lots of visitors called, such as parrots, cockatoos, and other strange birds of beautiful plumage, which kept up a continuous din. Families of small animals could be heard grunting and poking about. As the day broke we were entertained with a marvellous display of moths and brightly-hued butterflies, some measuring a foot across the wings.

We came upon a very pretty homestead next day. After receiving a hearty welcome they produced a large pot of tea for us. This is quite the usual custom. We swapped some pork for flour and a bag of tea and made some damper, otherwise called bread, to take on our journey. After a good chat we wished our hosts goodbye, taking our horses down the river for a good bogle or bath.

After that it was our turn for a wash and swim with the dogs. Herds of cattle, all shapes and sizes, came down to drink but our dogs played them up severely. First the cattle seemed to like having their own way, but the dogs persistently bossed them until worn out, they retired. The animals then came down with a great rush bringing all their friends with them.

By the time we reached Tower Hill, we were right out of provisions so when Tom went down to the creek. I went with my gun and dogs and bagged a brace of turkeys which made our position alright. After leaving the creek, the country, which had been flat with just plains and scrub, changed to rocks chasms and hills all round.

12

CAMP-FIRE TALES

Tom Tighe and I then continued on our 250 mile trek to Townsville by horseback accompanied by two useful dogs. At Ten Mile Bore, where we camped for the night, we were joined by a teamster with his yoke of 16 horses and wagon load of 10 tons of wool. Around the camp fire the talk turned to the discriminating intelligence of dogs. The teamster called for silence.

A Sagacious Australian Sheep Dog

"We had a dog called Ginger," he said, "she was a fair size lump of a bitch, very good with the monkeys, (that is, sheep). We were taking a large flock of 'em down the Barcoo when one night they broke away. It took nearly a week to round them up and even then we were 40 short.

"Being compelled to go on we decided to leave Ginger and a dog or two with full signs and instructions to follow on with the strays. Quite an ordinary procedure. Reaching our cattle station we soon forgot about them.

"Some months later we heard a commotion outside and saw a cloud of dust which heralded a flock of sheep, apparently in the charge of a dog or two only. When we yarded up the monkeys the leading dog came racing across for water.

"'Bless me if it isn't old Ginger!' we all exclaimed. It certainly was a bit of luck to get back our sheep, old Ginger and all. I guess that beats cock-fighting.

"Yes! But listen to this. Next morning we heard a commotion outside and saw a cloud of dust that heralded a flock of lambs and we thought we could just see our diamond brand growing on them. This made us think.

"Of course it was perfectly clear. They were the offspring of our 40 sheep and the pups that were driving them were the spitting image of our faithful and intelligent Ginger."

Our Educated Collies

Away down Warrogo River we halted with some valuable heifers. The Boss's son told us of an incident concerning his favourite collie.

"We were out with several mixed lots of cattle just after the rains and some of mine got lost. After spending a whole day rounding and sorting them out, I was still one short. I had an idea where the bullock was and I sent in my pet collie, 'Kangaroo'. to track it down and bring it in.

"As the time was getting on I rode down to see what the matter was. I did not want to lose the bullock and more particularly, Kangaroo, on whom I had devoted much time training him.

"After riding some time and whistling and shouting for him, I was rewarded with an answering bark. Still the dog did not appear. I pushed on through the marsh and rounding a bush I saw the dog was hard at work at something. I then noticed the head and neck of the bullock sticking out of a mud hole. The dog had a tin can in its mouth and pouring water over the bullock.

"And why was it doing that? Well it was perfectly clear.

"It was trying to wash the mud off the animal to see if it was ONE OF MY BRAND!"

Talking Skulls in a Crypt

Camping by Skeleton Creek, we were helped by a poor old man who was obsessed with "a b…b…black ghost" haunting him. I tried to help him with jokes and then I told him of the following awful affair.

Way down home at Bromley, some locals gathered in The Bell Tap pub. The talk soon got around to ghosts and spooks. Joe boldly stated that, "I don't believe in 'em and they will never scare me."

The Sexton of the Parish Church solemnly removed his tankard from his lips, took a deep breath, and with a withering look and severe tone said, "I will tell yer summit that'll make yer think. No man that ever handled a skull in our crypt, ever lived the year out.

"Skulls, skulls, poo!" sneered Joe.

"Yus. Hundereds of 'em stuck round the walls grinning at yer. I've seen 'em roll off the shelves groaning at yer. Ugh! I wouldn't touch one for a pension."

"Bet you don't fetch us one out, Joe," taunted Harry.

"How much?" shouts Joe.

"Five pounds," says Harry.

"Oh come, come," wheedles Joe, "make it ten pounds. All of you in the swim. Just two pounds each. A nice little Christmas box for me," coaxed Joe. "Stake it with the landlord."

Well, of course they could not back out of then. Two skulls were to be brought out at midnight.

The first stroke of the reverberating church clock was striking twelve. The sexton led the way down the icy steps followed stealthily by the other five. He turned the great key and opened the rusty and ponderous crypt door. All entered the dark chamber. The sexton halted and pressed back against a dank wall.

"Now!" he hissed, holding his lantern aloft.

Joe answered with a cough and willing hands urged him gently forward.

Heavens! Hark! A long drawn out howl filled the chamber. A lost spirit?

"W-what was that?" Joe chattered, shaking all over.

"N-n-nothing," the sexton blurted out, visibly affected. "Get on with it or pay up."

Joe, with trembling fingers, lit several matches. In the flickering light he observed several rows of grinning skulls. He stepped forward, shot out a hand to grab one when a deep sepulchral voice boomed, "That's mine!"

Very much shaken, Joe grabbed for another when the same voice groaned, "That's mine!" At the third attempt there was a repetition of the same tone, "That's mine!"

Joe, dropping the matches, manfully seized a skull in each hand and rushed for the steps.

"That be damned for a tale," he said, "Siamese twins if you like but not triplets with the same voice!"

Joe showed the skulls to his scared tormentors and collected his well earned wager.

13

TREKKING, CONTINUED

Seeing the outline of Tower Hill Station we hurried along hoping to replenish our larder. After nearly two hours of very difficult travelling we discovered that the Station was derelict. Turning away in disgust we missed the track entirely, but later on we observed an erection which proved to be a windmill pumping water. That was luck indeed for ourselves and our animals.

We next observed the chimney pots of a homestead away down in the valley, then saw a man and his wife on horseback galloping to meet us. After a ceremonious introduction they at once asked us to come in. It seemed a great pleasure to them to help us with various gifts.

We had a good meal and after a rest and chat we did our good turn by cutting up and dressing a sheep and rounding up horses for them. We slept inside their gates that night, and as we found that we were several miles off our road we got away with the break of day.

Of course this was the usual practice of early to bed and very early to rise, then away before the full heat of the day. From 11.30am to 3.30pm the animals and ourselves would have a feed and sleep provided we were lucky enough to find shade and water. Then on till dusk.

We found that the Farmers were keenly alive to the dangers of a prairie fire as the grass was as dry as tinder. We were often warned to be very careful. That day we returned to Tower Hill and climbed the hill from which the district is named. It is of curious formation with rocks straight up on its summit, like a castle.

At the top we found an iron plate inscribed: I.L. 19 Mch 1862. We ascertained that James Landsborough was the surveyor and one of the first white men that way. A large tree by the river also bears his name. Two additional important Britishers names can now be seen by all that can read.

We fell in with two fellows on horseback who had been moving their sheep to water. They invited us to their farm and the usual feed. The Mail Coach was expected down the Town and it was to be a Motor Mail Van. But sad to relate, it appeared with six horses in front and two behind. It appears that he ran into a gate post and tore a wheel off his van as well as doing other damage. So ended the first motor postal service over that route.

The Contractor went back to his horses again, amid the laughter and derision of the local inhabitants, who could see no good in those new fangled contraptions. But remember it was in the fairly early days of motoring, that is, 1921, and there were terrible roads.

We pushed on next morning away over the desert which here is 'desert' in name only. It consists mainly of rocky hills and sand and at times one runs into scrub and good-sized timber. It was late that night when we made camp although I had shot at a large turkey but the gobbler had won. Being dead tired we had a scratch supper and so went to bed.

Up again at daybreak we breakfasted and packed our few belongings. We decided to put in another long days trek to get away from the monotonous 'desert' lands. But our luck was dead out for our horses were nowhere to be seen, even though we had hobbled them. After searching for them, with our dogs, for some hours, they were still missing.

It now dawned on us the seriousness of our situation. We had no provisions and were scores of miles from any help. Our number one annoyance was that we were out of tobacco. Tom Tighe, however, had been experimenting with a mixture which almost wound up being fatal for him.

We next decided to foot it in opposite directions and reconnoitre for our horses. This may seem quite simple but there was always a big chance of being lost in the bush or desert. I have always been most cautious in taking bearings, and so on, much to the amusement of old hands. But I have had the satisfaction so far of never being utterly lost!

That is not bad for 'a Pommy'. One may ask what a Pommy is. Well, the New Chums are Emmigrants and this word rather curiously became 'Pomegranites' by some process and then Pommy for shortness.

Walking in the heat of the day was not my idea of enjoyment. Without a drink, without a smoke, and the anxiety of our position becoming intolerable, we had little hope of recapturing our horses. I made a long detour to circle and pick up the so-called main track again. Dejectedly I rested in the shade of a grand old tree, keeping my ears strained for the slightest sound of life.

What was that? Something!

I jumped up and ran then stopped dead and listened. Was it the roar of the wind of a bushfire coming our way? There was now a fearful rumbling, thundering noise like the sound of a heavy goods train, then I thought it now seemed to be like a charge of cavalry. Anyhow, it was right upon me!

Hundreds of pounding hoofs and clouds of dust was my next impression. I raced across the clearing and quickly climbed a useful tree. It was a mob of wild scrub bulls and cows, including a lot of miscellaneous animals, certainly not very pleasant for travellers to encounter, especially on foot, although on horseback it might be quite alright.

At length they passed and, just to relieve my feelings, I gave them a few earsplitting yells to help them on their way. I wondered what had disturbed them at a time when they would usually be resting in the shade. I sincerely hoped it was not a bushfire but there were no signs of that yet.

From my exalted and comfortable position I tried my lungs with occasional Coo-ee-s. In about a quarter of an hour I had an idea that I heard an answering call. Yes! My luck was in. The calls came nearer and soon I heard the shouts of a Teamster encouraging his horses and

I heard the crack of his mighty whip and the creaking of waggon wheels.

I shinned down from the tree to meet them. The wagoner gave me a cheerful salute and seemed to be looking behind me to see where my pals were hiding. I hopped up on the seat beside him, for it's difficult pulling up a team of horses only to start them again.

He asked me what the deuce I thought was doing there. He was making for Prairie.

I said, "For the love of Mike give me a smoke and a drink," and I pulled off my boots. I then felt a bit more merry and told him all about it, for we were really stranded.

"Look you here, boy," he said, "that's alright. If I like yer Camp we will stop, then we will see what can be done."

14

STILL TREKKING

With his help we picked up our site and after out-spanning and watering the horses, not forgetting our own comforts, he lent me a horse and saddle to go for a gallop in hopes of finding my horses. All ended well for I at once met Tom coming in with them. He had found them grazing close to where we had been in the morning.

There were two men working the Turnout, one was Cook, a chum of about 30, the other was a Horse Tailer, so weather-beaten that his age might be 45 or 75. They had a team of 28 horses and all the other hands had gone back by train after a 33-week drive with a flock of over 10,000 sheep.

They had no end of provisions, and they pressed us to join them. What a dinner we had. The Cook certainly was some Chef and he made a fine job of it and we passed him a fine compliment. Then some good coffee and a smoke to complete our contentment.

We travelled with them for some time, greatly to our advantage. I borrowed a spare cob and went off prospecting for some tobacco as they only had enough for themselves. I passed through pretty scenery and rocky gorges with deep chasms and waterfalls. I rode underneath one and came upon hundreds of kangaroos and rock wallabies on the other side.

I struck a homestead and got a quantity of tobacco. They were pleased to see me but were very upset because I would not stop for a feed and a few hours jaw about the world outside and London in particular. I had to tell them it was urgent for me to be on the go as my companions were not too pleased at my excursion at all. So I left the homestead with mutual regrets and thanks.

As it was, our outfit had pushed on and I had much trouble picking up their trail. I found them again at the next Bore, or water hole, and 'tucker' was ready and so was I. I got in their good books again when I doled out my tobacco.

Being early evening we tried some fishing but were not lucky which is usual in those parts. I did a bit of exploring down the bottom of some falls, an old custom of mine. I found some wonderful caves with beautiful tracery and brightly coloured objects of all description.

Hollowed in the floor was a beautiful red marble-like basin marked with strange symmetrical designs. In the clear water some large fish simply swarmed. I put in my arm to grab one when I was startled to find they swarmed up and nibbled my fingers. They appeared to be starving.

I worked my way up a shaft which appeared to have been burned black by volcanic action. When I struck full daylight again I noticed that my clothes and skin had been considerably damaged by the sharp rocks, and blood was running from my hands, face and knees.

On seeing me emerge Tom rushed to my aid and enquired what sort of monster I had been fighting in the bowels of the earth. When I explained he said he was unable to see sense in my adventures or rovings, and made some rude remarks about the state of my mind. He offered to knock some sense into me next time. In fact we came to blows there and then.

A few days before we had observed the signs of a bush fire many miles away. We now found it coming much closer with a following wind. Much as one would say after looking out of a window, "Looks like a storm is brewing up." The drovers said, "That's alright but we shall only out-span where there is a large clearing, the fire can run many miles in an hour."

That day was a long tiring trek and we were dead tired when we came to water. We gave scant attention to the drove, and after some tucker, we turned in and slept the sleep of the just. Our camp was on the outskirts of Skeleton Creek about two day's journey from our destination.

At some unearthly hour we were roused from our dreams by the drover shouting, "All hands on deck!" or something like it, with a few Australian love words chucked in. Then I heard, "Hurry up! The fire or summat is on us!" The dogs had gone crazy - 2 of ours and 6 of theirs - anyway there was a frightful racket and din and voices I did not recognise. I remember hollering, "Come along let's get to the Creek before we are cut off."

Being still half asleep I barged off and collided with two running figures and knocking one down in my haste. The other dropped some bundles and ran for his life with the dogs snarling and snapping at his heels. I certainly woke up then and flew after him getting the dogs under control at once.

As soon as we could make our voices heard above the din, we discovered that the two men were just season workers who were on their way to the shearing sheds. They always travel by night and work before the heat of the day.

We apologised profusely for the rough reception our guards (the dogs) had given them, and after filling them up with tea and damper (as is the rule of the road) they thanked us and departed into the star-lit night. After giving the Boss the 'bird' and a good dose of leg-pulling about his "Fire or summat", we turned in till morning.

Two days later we had a good clean up, washed and mended clothes. We did the same for ourselves and animals for there was much dilapidation both in body and raiments. We drove straight into the town of Prairie, and after some shopping we passed through and camped down the Creek. There was an old chap that joined us and helped with the horses.

"Damn glad to have some company," said he, "there was a b----- ghost round here! A b----- black ghost! Comes out in the pitch dark! No, I don't say it's a man and I don't say he ain't! A b----- black ghost!" he reiterated and shivered.

I could not imagine how he could see anything so adjectively black on a black night so I told him so. But he only continued sitting and hugging his head and repeating his song. I came to the conclusion that he was a bit mental and I tried to help him with a friendly chat and joke. I told him about a funny incident about ghosts and spooks in our Parish Church Vaults back home (Talking Skulls in a Crypt) but all to no purpose.

After a jolly evening in the Town, we wished them *au revoir*. We stayed in Prairie for a week and then I decided Tom Tighe was not the sort of Chum for me. I was fed up with his apathy and want of ambition. He quite agreed with my suggestion and we valued our stock. I took my half and quitted. I went to the Post Office and sent a wire to a chum called Bob that I would travel up and meet him in Townsville and join him in his trip to New Guinea.

15

FROM TREKKING TO PHOTOGRAPHY

At Augathella I fell in with a party of Drovers, Cowpunchers and the Owners who were on trek with a fine herd of pedigree heifers and bullocks. Like myself, they were making for South Queensland. I spent many jolly days in their company, and of course took a hand with the cattle, which numbered 985. We also had 19 horses, 2 buggies and 10 dogs.

I was riding Black Bess, which I had bought from Mr Curley Bell. She was conspicuously lovely even amongst the fine horses in those parts. But she was tricky and vicious, too, much like some of Curley's friends. Anyhow, I broke her in and I could do anything with her. Black Bess had been one of Curley's 'Star' buckjumpers in the Wild West Show.

'Open to all comers - £5 for a minute on Black Bess'. Trust Curley for knowing a good thing. He would pay out a fiver to the man who earned it, with a flourish of trumpets. But he had also made £50 in a single day, so 'docile' did the mare appear to be.

I had many a spree with some of her admirers when I had left her free outside an Hotel while I sampled their good *Moonstar* or *Emu Burgundy*.

"Want to try her, old boy?" I'd enquire. "Well, don't go far, I'm just off."

Then the fun began. Bess would snap, twist and rear as soon as a man attempted to touch a stirrup.

"Good gracious! Get away, you can't ride! What are you used to, an old moke?" I'd say.

A rider might throw himself into the saddle and then the fun began. Black Bess would neigh, rear on her hind legs and walk along pawing the air, then with a series of side jumps she would send the rider rolling in the dust.

Despite the yells of encouragement from the crowd of, "Stick to it chum!" Black Bess was seldom conquered for long. Then with a pat, a tap of the whip and a word from me she would lie down and I could make a pillow of her flank. She was as obedient as a child with me.

Passing through Charleville I picked up with Tommy Nightingale of Ellon Studios who was an Artist and Photographer. He hoped to make a living by painting and from photography.

"Business is very bad. Plenty of money about and people speak highly of my work but orders do not come in." That was his tale.

Next day I had a brain wave and looked in at the Studios. Tommy welcomed me and I said, "Tommy, how much will you give me in the pound on orders I bring in? I am a bit of a photographer myself you know."

"Oh," he said, "you can have half." Smiling mournfully he added, "You are up against it here!"

"Never mind the business outlook," I replied, "look out for business!"

I took a large 'group' he had just completed and showed it round at the Prince of Wales Hotel where I was staying (at Blackall) and in two days I had obtained so many orders for dozens and halves that Tommy abused me roundly. In artistic language and wreathed in clouds of smoke, he started off.

"Think I'm a blooming donkey to be worked day and night! There's enough there to keep me going for for the next three weeks! When am I going to do a bit of fishing?" he groused.

In the first week I cleared over £10, which included enlargements and colours. Later I got Tommy to strike out and travel. We purchased a buggy and a pair, I spent £5 on a camera, plates, dishes, hypo, bromide and so on. We made a picnic of it, had several smashes, found business good but difficult to transact, so we worked our way back to headquarters at Charleville again.

We then got our Country Orders, chiefly the new babies, the foal, the Homestead and The Governor and his Missus posing on the front door step. But our great stunt was to get in at the various Show Grounds where there was always good business with Prize Cattle.

Tommy had now cut out all the frills and we got on with the job. After acquiring a round sum of money, I was sitting thinking in the Tattersalle Hotel one night with Tommy, when all of a sudden, I just 'felt like it'. So I broke the news and Tommy's heart by saying, "I'm going trekking straight away tomorrow."

Despite Tommy's offer to make me a life partner in the business, find me a rich young wife, and other inducements, I bought out our buggy and pair, and was away on my own next morning at nine o'clock, heading for the never-never lands.

Shopkeeping was never a hobby of mine.

16

FROM PHOTOGRAPHY TO HUNTING

On reaching Townsville I met Bob and we decided first of all to go opossum hunting with my chum Syd Whittaker, and next day we started off towards Ayr.

Bob knew the country and was well up in the knowledge of our requirements. He was a good organiser, a fine horseman, and a dead shot. He showed me many tricks in the saddle also little stunts with the rifle which to the uninitiated was very bewildering. I was keen on all that sort of thing and became an apt pupil.

It was just the season to start opossum shooting and trapping. We had a good outfit, including three .22 Winchesters. We got right in amongst a school of opossums and with such good effect that we had to engage several Blacks to retrieve for us. The sight of these men was really wonderful. We soon secured a large quantity of skins which we sent direct into the Town, and it proved a very profitable undertaking.

One of our men, who we made foreman, was a Black tracker for the Queensland Police. He gave me a practical demonstration one day. We were riding along a dusty track when I said to him, "Peter, what time other yellow fellow leave camp, pass here?" (referring to a half-cast who had gone on ahead on foot.)

"Ah-h him yeller feller, longa-short-time here!"

"How do you know?" I said abruptly.

"Ah-h," said Peter with a you-don't-believe-me grin and showing the whites of his eyes. "Lookun you, Sir, vera plain, vera plain to see. His track right here see, lookun you!"

So, pulling up our horses I strained my eyes to where he was pointing and I could just distinguish a footprint. Sometimes when galloping along, Peter would brandish his arm and exclaim, "Lookun Sir, goanna, a big un, go-anna. lookun out longa tree." And he would point through the dense forrest trees to an iguana, way up in the branches.

The opossum season was now in full swing. We built a camp on the Annabranch River, and each day I went out with my dogs and men with snares and gun. We captured 80 a day. We had two months of mixed shooting and must have bagged over 5000 opossum skins alone.

The men were in my charge and I had much difficulty with them. The Blacks were always arguing with the Half-Casts, despite punishments I put on them. I found the only sure way was to scare them by telling them that, "The Devil was coming. The Devil will get you. Be quiet he's coming and I won't stop him". That had the desired effect.

The opposum season closed and I took a run to Bowen.

17

FROM HUNTER TO ACTOR

The first night I was in Bowen I made an appearance on the stage with Mr Sereck. Later on Mr Ferry (the Frog) and his wife pressed me to take a well paid job as Advance Agent representing several Theatrical Companies, to which I agreed.

While touring from Bowen to Townsville and Brisbane I had met many celebrated Actors and Actresses. I made many good friends and, on my visit to Ayr with the Ferrys, I got in with The Harry Clay Company, a very nice crowd. After them, Allan Wilkie came along with Shakespearean Plays.

That Sunday afternoon following we made up a party and motored down to Plantation Creek with our guns for some sport. We got right into a paddle of ducks and put up a flight of bandicoots. Then on to 'The Rocks' where we shot two wallabies and a crocodile.

The next Dramatic Company through my hands was The Ray Colonial Company, then doing pantomime. While staying at The Delta Hotel Mr Fred Francis and Miss Le Bane asked me to place some short sketches for them in the village of Tunir. As they were short-handed they persuaded me to give them some help and we all drove out together. I think it was lucky for them that I did so.

My advance work was well done for we had a bumper audience.

Unfortunately the Show was so poor and so short that serious trouble arose in the playhouse. As things looked so very awkward I decided to take the wind out of the sails of the ringleaders.

Rushing up on stage I quietly informed the gathering that there was some amongst them that did not know what pleasure was in store for them. This appeared to be a unique Show for Queensland. It was actually one of those Popular London Cabaret Nights. They had had a capital musical introduction and now Dancing until Midnight would begin and there would be handsome Prizes. Acting as Master of Ceremonies I shouted, "Take your partners!"

The Aussies never can resist dancing so they went on with it. Skilfully passing the reins on to the locals we slipped away one by one, taking our heavy cash bag round to a distant tavern where we spent a couple of hours celebrating our good luck.

When we thought our patrons had gone home we crept back to the Hall and paid off the caretaker. Then we spent a very uncomfortable night, the ladies sleeping under the stage while we parked ourselves amongst the stage effects on the top, making up beds with the chairs.

The next day I journeyed on to Ayr where I had some good business. Then back again to my old spot at Bowen where I featured in *The Land of the Living*. That was at The Star Theatre. Mine was quite a leading character, the Villain of the Piece, and I was complimented on my success. With me was Fred Francis and Miss Le Bane. We continued to play in Halls and Theatres, some small, others very big, right away from Townsville, Ayr and Bowen, right down to Mackay, Barcaldine, Blackall and Brisbane.

At the conclusion of our successful tour, I formed my own Company which I named The Frisco Strollers. Our fame preceded us and we passed from one success to another, appearing before crowded houses.

I will record the *Dramatis Personae*:- George Farnum otherwise Archie Filby, Ferry the Frog, Francis Gilmore, Bessie Lester, Pearl Shaddon, Harry Denver, Fred Francis, Connie Le Bane, Roy Nelson, Joe Peary, and others.

After 32 weeks of sound business we disbanded, some going off to China, others to America and Europe.

While I was staying at The Grand Austral Hotel, I met Miss Yvonne Banyard, the Leading Lady in a successful Company called Your Own Company. It was a good cast and we played *The Guilded Cage*, *The Sign on the Door* and *Bought and Paid For*. Mr Harrington Reynolds was the Business Manager and I was Advance Representative. Both of us, however, usually took part in the shows. The gowns worn by Miss Yvonne Banyard were supplied by Poiret and Panquin of Paris, the hats by Gage.

I next took the post of Manager of His Majesty's Theatre, Brisbane and my Headquarters was The Theatre Royal Hotel.

Theatre Managing involved long hours of hard work and I was glad when my contract expired. I soliloquised, *only fools and horses work land. Indeed, what was the sense of making £50 per week if it cost me £51?*

I decided to pop down to Bowen for a rest at the invitation of some friends. I have a soft spot in my heart for the Sleepy Hollow as Bowen is often called. It is a very pretty place and most sociable. I make a point of staying there whenever I am that side of Queensland. Sometimes I arrive there by train, at others by motor car, motor cycle, horseback or buggy.

The harbour is a natural picture, with its palms and fruit trees circling above the multicoloured rocks. Choice fruit-growing and copper-smelting are among its chief industries. Now that coal has been discovered in paying quantities, a big future is predicted for this attractive port.

18

FROM ACTOR TO HOTEL REPRESENTATIVE

At the finish of my theatrical engagements in Brisbane, I received an invitation to take up the advertising and boosting of The Wentworth Hotel and Cafe, probably the most popular House in Sydney. The proprietor offered me most liberal terms and a free hand. It appealed to me and I accepted.

Starting with some elaborate Dances and novel Cabaret Shows, the House was soon filled to capacity every night. The Boss, however, did not appear to be really satisfied!

"I must have something different, out of the ordinary, sensational," he said. "Look here, Filby, you said you could do it! I don't care what it costs!"

"Right ho!!" I replied. "I'll fix that up for you. Leave it to me."

I drove round to my friend, Captain Percival, a flying pilot at the Mascot Aerodrome, and made a bargain. Then I called upon a lady with whom after a long and secret talk, we arranged to put on a novel stunt that would put The Wentworth right on the map. Advertisements were put in *The Sydney Sunday Times, The Sydney Sun, The Sydney Evening News*, etc.:

THE WENTWORTH HOTEL AND CAFE, SYDNEY

The Management of THE WENTWORTH, Sydney's leading Cafe, have great pleasure in announcing the engagement at great cost of the famous Dance Band "THE NEW ORCHESTRA".
In addition to this Notice we are glad to be able to announce that we have concluded an agreement with Mr Archie Filby, the Actor and well known Theatrical Manager, who will produce A MYSTERIOUS AND BEAUTIFUL MASKED DANCER. This lady will arrive by Plane at The Mascot Aerodrome at 7.45pm precisely on Wednesday 3rd February 1926.
WHO IS SHE?
Not until the close of THE DANCE SEASON will her identity be disclosed then she will unmask in the WENTWORTH BALL ROOM. THE MYSTERIOUS DANCER will appear in her original creation nightly: HER DANCE FANTASTIQUE!!!
A MYSTERIOUS LADY, THE MASKED DANCER, WILL COME DOWN FROM THE SKIES IN A SERIES OF GRAND FANCY DRESS BALLS AT THE WENTWORTH!
A special engagement for thirty days only!
THIS MYSTERIOUS AND LOVELY WOMAN, MASKED AND IN PINK TIGHTS, DROPPED DOWN FROM THE BLUE WITH THE CASUAL EASE OF A BIRD.
ONLY HER ASTUTE MANAGER, MR ARCHIE FILBY FROM LONDON, HOLDS THE MUCH SOUGHT AFTER SOLUTION TO HER IDENTITY."

The Press seized on this tit-bit and came out in flaring headlines:

The Sydney Sun (4th Feb 1926):
"Great interest was aroused when Captain Percival brought down his aircraft on the runway of The Mascot Aerodrome on Wednesday last. He made a perfect landing in spite of the high wind. A large crowd had gathered as it was known that he brought a Special Passsenger: THE MYSTERIOUS AND BEAUTIFUL MASKED DANCER. This young woman was

welcomed to Sydney by Mrs Maclurkan. The Masked Lady then left the aerodrome accompanied by Mr Archie Filby her astute Manager from London. Mr Filby then drove her through the crowd (in his presentation Vauxhall) to the Wentworth Hotel where she received a very hearty welcome. During the evening she gave a marvellous display in her wonderful interpretation of the Art of Terpsichore entitled "THE VAMPIRE".

The Sydney Sunday Times:
"The Masked Dancer who showed off her pink tights and leg agility made a dramatic descent on the jaded and bored of Sydney. Mr Archie Filby, her manager and Agent, has brought us something "that will make us sit up and take notice": Aviator Captain Percival piloted the mysterious woman - masked and wearing a swish aviation suit of cream gaberdine, with a close fitting cap jammed over a glittering shingle - and dropped down from the blue with the casual ease of a bird alighting. Wild guesses are going round as to who she is. Some of the bright lads of the village have offered to escort her home in hopes of unravelling the mystery."

The Sydney Evening News:
THE MASKED LADY in a totally different act at THE WENTWORTH TO-NIGHT.
Nobody but her astute Manager knows who she is or where she comes from. Everybody studies the outline of her square chin, her carmined lips and the outline of her cute figure - but a month hence she will unmask, and if she sustains the wonderful interest excited by her advent then that popular rendezvous The Wentworth Hotel and Café will be packed for the dènoument.

Crowds besieged the ticket offices, although we doubled and redoubled the prices. We had to put up a large marquee to cope with Dinners and Suppers, etc. that went on until the early hours of the mornings.
The advent of THE UNKNOWN MASKED DANCER was

without doubt a huge success, for the Proprietor admitted that his House had obtained more publicity than even he had expected. At the close of the Winter Season, I reluctantly bid adieu to The Wentworth Hotel.

19

FROM HOTEL REPRESENTATIVE
TO REALTY DEVELOPMENT

I next renewed the acquaintance of Mr Reginald Oats by telephone at Brisbane. It took but a few minutes to come to an agreement, and the following week I entered the palatial offices on the corner of Queen Street and George Street. The firm's title was: The Oates Estate and Realty Development Company Limited.

With my new Hudson Essex car, I spent most of the time speeding about the district and fixing up deals of land and property. I soon found, however, that I was looked upon as The New Manager. Being very busy in the office one day and pressed for time, I was greatly interrupted by what they described themselves as "a deputation from the Staff". The spokesman stated that they had grievances in regard to Wages, Hours and Other Things.

To get rid of them, at least for the time being, I, as I thought, said rather humorously, "Oh yes. Certainly if you want to strike as you suggest, I really should. Do you want me to give you a lead? Come and see me tomorrow!"

Anyhow, I got rid of them without having a row and the next thing I heard was, 'The New Manager from London was organising a strike and was leading it!'

Curiously enough I happened to be a bit disgruntled over some sums I had reckoned I was entitled to in connection with sales. Some of the men explained to me their case, and I there and then agreed to be Strike Leader in earnest. I engineered the affair which went on for a week. The strike caused a tremendous stir in Brisbane, and fear was expressed that it might spread to other businesses.

At the weekend the Partners met us handsomely and work was resumed. We became closer friends than before. At the end of a few months I had accumulated several hundred pounds and was feeling that I must be up and off again 'North'.

I had my heart set on a long run right away up the Northern Territory, almost unmapped country, via Victoria, New South Wales, and Queensland to Cape York across the Torres Straits to Thursday Island. By chance I mentioned my ideas to the Manager of MotorCars Ltd George Street Brisbane, the outcome was that I resigned from Messrs Oates at the month end.

MotorCars Ltd Manager said, I could represent them "as Northern Traveller". The Company had been waiting for the right man for a long time. The terms were satisfactory and I motored away thousands of miles calling at most towns and villages *en route*.

20

TOURING IN NORTHERN QUEENSLAND

[The following article appeared in a Motoring journal called THE STEERING WHEEL on February 1, 1924.]

TOURING IN NORTHERN QUEENSLAND - AN
INTERESTING TRIP - BY A. E. FILBY.

I arrived in Mackay on the *Wyraema* and waited for my Essex car to arrive by train, which it did in good condition, and was soon off the truck and purring merrily toward the Grand Hotel.

Whilst in Mackay I visited Sarina which is back along the road to Rockhampton. It is only a country track but in very fair condition. I also visited Walkerston, Plaistowe, Marion and all the small towns round about, there being quite a number of them, as there are seven mills.

The country was suffering very much from the lack of rain. The only place that looked fresh was a certain Chinaman's garden. But it was found after a while that he had used the town supply by digging underground and getting on the pipe, then watering his garden by night.

Two places of interest which should not be missed by a visitor to

Mackay are Eimeo, which is about twelve miles from town on a fair road. There is a very good hotel here and views are wonderful, a large avenue of trees leading up to the foot of a sharp incline, which can be climbed easily by a good car. From the top one can see inland over the palms and other tropical vegetation, while on the other three sides a beautiful panorama of beaches are to be seen, the bathing being wonderfully good.

The other spot is the Rocks, which are not far from Eimeo. It is, as its name implies, a mass of picturesque rocks, and well worth seeing. The road leading to it is very soft sand and should only be attempted by a car that can pull.

I left Mackay early in the morning after saying goodbye to the many friends I had made and got well on the road to Proserpine before it got too hot, the road being very good until I got to The Leap, which is part of a high range of hills which are sheer on one side. A story is told of an Aboriginal, flying from the police, who jumped to his doom in the valley below rather than be taken by them.

The driver of any kind of car on this road is kept well occupied as there are over one hundred rivers or creeks on the ninety-five mile run. Several of the creeks want looking at by a stranger to the road as in some of them the road follows along the river bed before going up the other side. One annoying thing I noticed was I was minus my spare wheel, owing to it not have been put on properly when leaving. I had to go back twenty miles and found it resting blissfully against a tree.

Prappi is the only habitation on the road except the homestead, which is half way to Proserpine. When entering the river, I went straight down and up the other side instead of following the river, much to the surprise of the workmen working on the new railway bridge, as the climb on the other side is exceptionally sharp.

There were several railway construction camps on the road and in several cases the railway line cuts across the road and a wire fence is being put up so the road has to follow alongside and cross probably some distance from where it originally did, but it is easy to follow.

On entering Proserpine I went to Kelly's Hotel and was made very comfortable there in spite of the fact that the town was rapidly filling for show week. The roads around Proserpine are very good and the scenery very interesting. The beaches are also very pretty.

A little excitement is supplied by alligator shooting. I shot one three miles from the town, 15ft. 6in. long. Barramundi spearing is also a popular sport here.

I started for Bowen but as there had been several arguments as to whether the Essex could do the petrol consumption under the conditions prevailing up there, I undertook to take a party across with me. Miss Grace Severie, Miss Henderson, Mr Crawford and Mr Ross and Mr Hallam accompanied me.

The manager of the A.C. Bank [CommBank] was good enough to to see the tank filled and then sealed it with bank seals. After hearing from everyone we could not get through, let alone do any sort of petrol consumption, we started.

The first river certainly did look a puzzle as the ground simply disappeared from the front of the car and I was under the impression that we had taken the wrong track and the road must be somewhere else. Mr Hallam got out and found the road was down the bank and then along a stretch of loose sand. The rest of the company volunteered to get out to lighten the load but I thought this would be a good time to show exactly what the car will do, so went down the first bank and up the other side without anybody getting out.

After this the road was in a frightful condition, wash-aways occurring every few yards, with every kind of obstacle that is possible, and on top of this it had rained hard the previous night, so the creek approaches were very slippery, while some of the clay parts made it hard to keep straight. The road after this improved and was fairly good except for one bad creek.

On arriving in Bowen, the manager of the A.C.B. Bank and Mr Magee came down and checked the seals on the tank, and saw the consumption measured, which worked out at nearly 28 miles to the gallon, which was exceptionally good, considering the bad roads over which we had come. I must tend my thanks to the manager of Proserpine and also at Bowen, for the help they gave me.

The road from Bowen to Homehill is again very bad in parts, although passable to a fair driver and a good car that is not too heavy.

One passes through Bobbawobba and several other small sidings before arriving at Homehill. This town is going ahead in fine style, an irrigation plant being now in full swing. The plant also supplies the town with electric light. One now has to truck [send by train] the car across the Burdekin River to Ayr, as it is practically an impossibility to cross, although it has been done, but the shifting quick-sands make it too big a risk to attempt.

On entering Ayr I was struck by the number of cars there, conditions being very favourable. Owing to the roads being fairly good, the tyre mileage is exceptional. The spot well worth visiting here is the Anabranch River, where a very pleasant time can be spent with good fishing and wallaby shooting, and if one has taste for oysters they are there to be picked up.

The road from there on to Townsville I found very good, the Hawke River, which proves a bug-bear to many cars, being negotiated without any trouble, the car pulling very well through the sand and up the other side in great style.

I now came to the paradise of the north for motors, Townsville, the roads being all tar and kept in very fine condition. Townsville is exceptionally pretty, and the people I met there are very hospitable, going out of their way to make one feel at home. Through the courtesy of Mr Horn, I was able to secure some very fine games of golf on the pretty links there. The heat is not so bad as it is painted, the main town certainly being very hot, but if one stays at one of the three hotels on the front, it is very pleasant, especially at the Queen's, which is one of the finest in the North.

The road to Charters Towers is fairly good, except the Oakey Creek and over the range. Charters Towers is a much bigger place than I have been led to expect with good roads and pretty scenery around it.

On the return trip to Townsville, I drove a Hudson Super Six, which went over the range in great style. On our arrival at Oakey Creek we found several cars well stuck in the soft sand. One car had been there nearly two hours, as it had got off the right track and was in the sand over the hub caps, the differential resting on the sand, with the result the wheels were just spinning. I got a long pole and chock and lifted both wheels on to some strips of bark, and had the car out in under three minutes. We then gave the others a hand out and I came across with the Hudson without the slightest trouble.

Mr Donovan came with me to Ingham, also Mr Walker, Deputy Chief Engineer for Queensland. The road to Ingham from Townsville is very rough in places, the Blue and Black Rivers having very rough entrances and exits, also Salt Water Creek. We stopped at Rolling Stone for lunch, and then on to Ingham, doing the trip comfortably in five hours.

I spent a few weeks in Ingham as the guest of Mr and Mrs Whittaker, who showed me all round the country, the roads being in a very bad condition indeed. I should say here that the only voluntary stop on the whole trip was a puncture, caused by going over a nail in one of the bridges, all of which give one the impression that they will fall through before the car can get to the other side.

The most interesting part of the journey now commences. There are two routes between Ingham and Cardwell, one over the top of the Cardwell Range, the other seven miles further, but a good road round the foot of the range. It is absolutely necessary that anyone going over should have a good pulling car, and good brakes, as the incline is very sharp in places, and a run backwards would mean the end of things, as there is nearly a sheer drop on one side, while the bank is on the other, but like all things that are hard to get the climb is well worth it, the view from the top being wonderful, the Hinchinbrook Channel seeming to lay out at one's feet, with the numerous islands dotted all over the seascape.

I was unfortunate in being unable to get photos, but just as I had decided to take some, I found that a bush fire which I had noticed coming home, was getting much too near to be pleasant, the flames running along the dry grass and creepers and catching the dead palm fronds with astonishing rapidity. The descent was very steep and good brakes are wanted to attempt it.

I stayed the night at the Cardwell Hotel, and left for the Tully River after picking up Mr Atkins and Mr Savill, of the Lass o' Garry. The road on to the Tully River is very fine indeed, crossing the new construction line several times. Care has to be taken as the creeks are deep and fairly numerous. We nearly had a nasty smash at one of them, as one is apt to think they are the only car on the road, the result being that I nearly met a construction lorry at the bottom of one of the creeks, who was also thinking the same as myself, that a good run down would help up the other side. We were informed before leaving that the only way across the Tully River was to go to the sawmill and get them to ferry us across.

This I did, the ferry being a sampan or banana boat with boards put across from side to side and then two planks put parallel on top. I had to go down a very steep bank and get the wheels on to the two planks. This I succeeded in doing with the result that we got an exact balance instead of being slightly on one side, so that we could stand on the other and keep her on an even keel.

Every time we moved we swayed perilously from side to side. This, however, was the least of our troubles, for the owner of this strange craft informed us in the most casual voice in the world that she had sprung a leak.

A wild cry from Mr Savill informed us how bad things were, while Mr Atkins jumped to the rescue with a kerosene tin and started bailing out as hard as he could go. This sudden movement nearly upset us in 20ft. of water.

As I could not get back off the boards and up the bank I gave the order forward and we attempted to go straight across instead of downstream a bit first, which was the correct crossing. But on getting to the other side the anchor would not hold, so we circled slowly round and round, gradually getting lower and lower.

During one of these turns we came near the bank, and Mr Savill jumped ashore, at the same time saying, "Take a jump" to the car. As the water was now coming in little waves over the sides, I started the engine and took a chance, just landing, fortunately, in about a foot and a half of water. The sudden start pushed the planks backwards and knocked the back of the boat, which immediately sank out of sight, as the bank shelved sharply.

The engine pulled the car up on to the sand with the aid of a couple of planks, and then started a heavy pull through about 100 yards of loose sand with a steep bank at the end of it. With the rest of the party giving a helping hand, I got to the bottom of the bank.

The man in charge told me he would use the windlass that was erected at the top of the bank with the express purpose of pulling cars up the bank. But while he was going up I had a go at it on low gear, and with a bit of a struggle, arrived at the top, much to his surprise. He informed me that this was the first car that had ever been up under its own power since he had been there, which is somewhere about eight years, so I think we can safely say it was the first. Now came the biggest struggle of the whole lot - that was, paying £3 for being nearly drowned.

By the time we were over, it was getting dark, but Mr Atkins was in a hurry to push on to Innisfail, as some of the telegraph pole holes required looking at. We pushed on, the road following the river bank for some distance. We repeatedly had to retrace our course as the railway fence had been erected across the road. As on the Proserpine road, a new track had to be made alongside.

The next stop was at the Banyan Post Office where we had supper with the postmaster and Dr Cameron. Then, as it was a beautiful moonlit night, we elected to push on. The road was in a very fair condition for a while except for occasional stretches.

Then a strange thing happened. We came on one of the construction camp towns and by the sound of things someone was having a party. When we approached, however, everyone seemed to have fallen asleep at once, probably thinking we were police officers looking for the source of merriment.. After a great deal of shouting, a Chinaman came out and asked what the trouble was, but it was very evident that he wished to get rid of us. On my request for accommodation he said it was impossible and that Elrish [El Arish] was a short way over the "Little Bump". So we went on our way over a very bad road and found the "Little Bump" was the Tam o' Shanter Range.

It was the most beautiful sight, palms, orchids, etc., being on every hand, all being traced against the sky by a wonderful moon. We nearly had a nasty accident when near the top, as the road, curving sharply, had on one side a sheer wall, while on the other is a drop of 500ft.

While taking this hill I nearly omitted to take a corner, with the result that we almost took a leap into the valley below, but with a quick turn of the wheel we got round, although I think most of us were a bit shaky after it. We stopped a few seconds to admire the wonderful view, then on down the other side through several running creeks and some of the most beautiful scenery I have seen in Australia.

On our arrival at El Arish we woke someone up, who gave us a cup of tea and fixed us up with a shake-down, and informed us that they thought we were a bit mad to attempt the Tam o' Shanter Range by night.

In the morning, owing to the courtesy of the station master, we were able to secure a truck [train] as there was no road at all through to Innisfail, the bridges all being burnt and the scrub being all grown up in the track, although one can get as far as Silkwood a few miles on. We went there but found the truck was at El Arish, so we returned and loaded. While on the subject of loading trucks, a tip that is useful is load backwards, as a car will swing the front wheels much quicker than the rear.

Innisfail, although at one time having the second biggest rainfall in the world, is one of the driest places as far as water is concerned I have ever seen. The dust is something awful, cars having to travel with lights on during the day. There is hardly any water to be got, the Chinese laundries even being closed down. Innisfail is wonderfully pretty and one of the wealthiest towns for its size in Queensland. The Main Roads Board, having started work, should have some fine roads here. A spot worth visiting is Flying Fish Point where a pleasant time can be spent fishing and swimming, Mourilyan Harbour and South Johnstone being also well worth a visit.

After saying goodbye to the many good friends I had made here, I started off for Babinda with Mr J Bodkin with me. After crossing the Daradgee Ferry the road is fairly good as far as Eubenangee, but after this the motorist is well advised to truck his car. The road practically finishes here, but we continued on, the first trouble being tree stumps, which were too high to get the car over, so we had to build each side for the wheels to run up and so clear the car. We next struck a bridge across the railway which is the only good part of the road.

The next five miles are wonderfully pretty but rather trying to the driver, the road being practically a tunnel through the tropical undergrowth which comes right up on both sides and also right down on the hood, Mr Bodkin frequently having to get out to move the vine or creeper that barred our progress. The hills are very sharp and washaways running down the centre usually have the car at a perilous angle, while fallen trees often have to be built over or another track made round them.

Our next diversion on the route was some very bad gullies, which had been corduroyed some years ago, but now are in an awful state of repair. It is quite easy to lose one's way at Waugh Pocket, as the road looks tempting to the left, but you have to follow the telegraph line. The road has been corduroyed with eight inch logs and the ants and bush fires have destroyed one in every four so that at every 3ft. there is an 8in. drop. This continued for about four miles, as it is impossible to miss it, as a scrub comes down on both sides.

After a few very sharp pulls with bad surfaces, one strikes the Russell River. The river is quite passable but on the other side there is a very sharp bank of sand that is impossible to climb, although I believe if the river is followed upstream it might be done. Unfortunately I went straight across and found that, while the wheels were still on the level the dumb irons were touching the bank so there was no chance of getting up. I borrowed a few horses and soon had her out, then on, and within a few hundred yards comes the Josephine.

A peculiar thing happened here. There is a sharp lip out of the water, then a steep climb. I went across and up about 4ft. but thought the rear wheels had not cleared the lip, so went back in the water for a second run. Water from the car, however, had wet the clay bank and made it too slippery for the wheels to grip. We had to wait for the sun to dry it before making it over.

After this the road is good right into Babinda. I stopped at the Babinda State Hotel which is one of the best in the district. After staying the night I went onto Gordonvale and then on to Cairns. The roads on the tableland are all pretty good and the towns all worth a visit. Of course every visitor goes to see the Barron Falls. At this time of the year there is very little water falling. Another pretty spot is

Double Island, which is about 12 miles from Cairns, on a fair road, with pretty scenery, especially from the Barron River.

On my return from Cairns to Townsville I did the journey in 14½ hours actual running time, having Mr H Christmas on board from Cairns to Innisfail, crossing the Josephine without trouble, then the Russell. I took a run at the bank and slid sideways down and was soon across, having a no-trouble run to Innisfail over a road which is very trying to the springs.

After this I trucked to El Arish again, and picked up a couple of land buyers and luckily took them with me, as I found when I got to the top of the Tam o' Shanter Range. Bush fires had been playing havoc, there being trees across the road in quite a number of cases. We managed to roll them over in to the valley below, there being a sheer drop on one side.

At the same place that we nearly went over before, there was a half-burnt tree stump of considerable dimensions, which came off the hill above us and caught the back of the car, having us nearly over the edge. I was carrying some important documents for the police which had to be in Townsville at a certain time.

Crossing the Tully, I took a lower crossing and with a bit of a struggle, the car going well into the water, I crossed O.K. It is wonderful the way in which the Tully River settlement has grown since I came through, there now being four stores and everything in full swing, getting ready for the coming of the new mill.

We made good time between the Tully and Cardwell. Stopping a few minutes in Cardwell, I went round the Cardwell Range, the whole of the scrub being on fire, also a few of the bridges. I crossed one at full speed that was burning nicely and on going a few miles further, found one that was completely burned. I must tend my thanks to the workmen on the railway construction, who came up and chopped a couple of fair-sized trees down and put them across the gulley. I ran across these two with a wheel on each.

I soon arrived in Ingham without any further trouble, although the fires came unpleasantly close at times. After reporting at the Police Station, so they would check the time and also that the documents were safe, I picked up Mr Whittaker.

It was noticeable the creeks that had been running before were now dry. With a short stop at Rollingstone, we made a no-trouble run to Townsville in four hours. I left the car in Townsville, having tried it out on every class of country, and returned to Brisbane.

Some time later I crossed to Dutch Papua, New Guinea and the Solomon Islands, also Flinders Island, Tasmania, New Zealand, and Samoa. Much of the latter journeys were accomplished on Motor Cycle with side car. Ordinary cars were out of the question as often roads did not exist.

21

A VISIT TO TASMANIA (1925)

At the conclusion of many months of travel in Australia I reached Brisbane once again. After mapping out a plan I took a train to Melbourne and spent a few days visiting the Shrine of Remembrance, the palatial Public Buildings and Parks. The Melbourneites are very proud of their city and I think that they are justified in doing so.

At the Imperial Club I met Captain Donald, the owner of a yacht. When I mentioned that I wanted to pop over to Tasmania for a day or two, he immediately offered to sail me there. So, of course, that was that! We left Port Phillip and sailed away across the Bass Straits, calling at Flinders Island to try out their famous beer.

With a stiff breeze we appeared to be making good time and anyway we had a good time. All took their share of the work and in about a week we made Devonport after a very interesting voyage which I calculated to be about 500 miles.

"Now, Captain," I said, "before we part, I am going to celebrate the voyage with a dinner at the Hotel."

They were all up for it and up we went. I called for the best Tasmanian wines and liqueurs and we toasted each other again.

"Now, Captain," I said, "just a little private business. How much am I indebted to you for the last eight days, etc."

"I am the Skipper," said he, "and I will first put this dinner on the bill and then we will see about it."

Despite my friendly protestations he refused to take a penny from me for the voyage or the expenses incurred. It was still early evening when I wished them *adieu*, so I mounted my motor cycle which I still clung to and put its head towards Launceston.

The last words of Captain Donald was, "Look you Phill, let me know when you return to the mainland and I will be along and sail you back."

"Right oh, thanks, I won't forget. Ta Ta."

I carried letters of introduction to some Smiths at Launceston and on my arrival they made me welcome and put me up for the night. I found that they were all interested in motor racing, one of the chief sports on the island. We found we had much in common and I was soon one of the party and took part in motor racing and other stunts.

This led me to more expert work up on the Wynyard racing track. I secured several awards and went in for long distance racing and cycle and car tests, both on the track and the excellent roads.

We had some fine outings. We climbed Ben Lomond, 5000 feet up, just for a little picnic. We visited the freshwater fish reserve set apart by the ichthyologists for intensive study. we went to the workings of 'Tasmanite' which is a most curious reddish sort of shale. Although resinous, it is insoluble in benzine, alcohol etc.

Tasmania grows an aromatic evergreen shrub with leathery dotted leaves, very pungent and its fruit is made into a kind of pepper.

My pals very often said to me you really must see Van Diemans Land before you go, if you like Tasmania. We are sure you will be delighted with Van Diemans Land. Of course I was all for it. This went on for some time until I accidentally discovered that it was a leg pull at my expense. I found that the island was so called until 300 years ago when it was rediscovered by Abel Tasman.

The Island is very attractive and covers an area of about 250 miles by 500 miles. The fruits and flowers are glorious and it is hard to believe the scenes of ice and snow that were shown to me in pictures.

Again weeks late on my itinerary, I wished my Tasmanian friends *au revoir*. I took the regular shipping service from Hobart Town to

Columbo. Chatting in the saloon one night, the conversation turned to yachting. I startled my companions and myself by shrieking out, "Dash it all! Yachting, yachting. There is Captain Donald waiting to bring me in his yacht from Tasmania. I clean forgot it!"

I often think of Tasmania, a lovely island. Oh, the glorious Tasman cider, my people at home would appreciate it!

22

A REMARKABLE ADVENTURE BY MOTOR COMBINATION

I travelled away on a most remarkable journey through the Cape York Peninsular and Thursday Island. I came in touch with primitive man. The black Aborigines. Cannibals. Warring tribes. Anthrapoid apes, and groups so unintelligent that they would scramble into holes and climb trees at our approach.

I purchased a powerful motor cycle with sidecar, and took Curley Bell for a long run up North, stopping at Townsville and Muttaborough. Then on to Woollansmarroo and Cooktown, passing through weird and virtually unmapped country.

At Cooktown we had a rest for a few days, a curious cosmopolitan place. The 3,000 inhabitants consisted of Jews, Russians, Turks, Syrians, French, Greeks, Chinese, etc. They looked an unshaven ragtag and bobtail crowd of casual workers. Well, that is how they appeared to me at first. I discovered later that the untrimmed whiskers covered many a notabilities countenance, such as priest, magistrate, lawyer, and stationmaster.

The shops were small and puny. On the fishmonger's slab I noticed a dozen sprats spread out, while the Jap owner lolled half-asleep on the door step. Few had the energy to keep upright, preferring to lean against a post or sink to the ground, where they would chatter or have a gamble together in the main street, which was strictly forbidden.

The Italian saloon and *maison de jeu* man pulled himself to his feet as we approached, and soothingly bowed to us, saying, "*Un petit gueme billiards, Monsieurs?*"

"*Qui, qui, Monsieur,*" I replied, returning the bow.

Curley and I went in and knocked the balls round the antiquated table with barge poles for cues. Then in my best Parisian French I ordered chalk, drinks, cigars, sandwiches, etc. This seemed to annoy the Italiano-Frenchie exceedingly, for he blurted out, "Speak English, damn you, I lived in Charing Cross Road!"

Shortly after, a donkey came up the steps and nibbled our clothes. Instead of kicking the donkey, who might be a 'god' of the proprietor, we decided to go to the water front and have a swim. Inside the Great Barrier Reef the sea was perfectly clear, shoals of fish disported themselves, they made a fascinating spectacle. They ranged from the mighty manta ray and barracuda to the brilliant coloured small fry.

In our hotel we noticed an uncouth looking jail bird, in the bar at all hours of the day and night, who seemed to get great respect and unlimited free drinks. We were told he was the Police Captain and, "We had better stand him one and give him a tip or we might be arrested."

"Arrested!" remonstrated Curly, "what for?"

"Oh nothing," said our informant, "just nothing."

We got on alright with 'His Highness' who between hiccoughs apologised "that the prison was full up."

Cooktown is a go-as-you-please place, dress or undress as you like. Your goats, chickens, mokes or nags, push them out with the children to forage for themselves. Don't be caught working or you may become unpopular. That somewhat true adage - 'only fools and donkeys work' - undoubtedly came from Cooktown.

Curley Bell, having finished his business in Cooktown, repaired to the railway station, where I saw him off to Brisbane. We noticed the Police Captain swaggering out of the hotel opposite, as he had been sent for. Two stowaways on the train were then handed to him. The last I saw of them was the Captain forcibly propelling his prisoners over to the bar.

I now set to equip myself for the further run up to Cape York, the Northern most point of Australia. From there I should cross the Torres Straits to Thursday Island, the centre of the pearl fishing grounds.

It would be no easy run, I would be by myself for 700 miles, in most of the distance the roads were practically non-existent. Petrol and provisions had to be carefully budgeted and a decent and safe place to stay the nights was essential. Troublesome natives and dangerous animals were really few but herds of wild horses, a drift of swine, or even a pack of dingoes can easily disturb one's comfort and safety.

Actually I found the roads much worse than what I had been told, I was really surprised that my outfit withstood the contortions put upon it. A strange country, bush scrub, sand, rocks and water, but quite interesting. Now and then a fair-sized village. The journey is usually made by the Burns Phillips Steamers, but I was precluded from that as I had a business call or two to make inland.

I found I was well behind my schedule so to make up time I tried several short cuts. One night I went along a single railway. The line continued across a high temporary bridge over a river seething with crocodiles. That in itself was not pleasant. The single narrow gauge only left me about a foot to spare on each side of my combination. I had proceeded 50 yards across bumping from sleeper, walking with the engine just ticking over when I heard the whistle of a train evidently making for the bridge then I saw by the reflection in the sky that it was about half a mile away. I must get back again and quickly!

Can you imagine the excitement I was in pushing that heavy cycle and sidecar backwards to reach the bank I had just left? I did some quick thinking - I knew the train would beat me! Should I let the machine go into the river? I could easily hang on underneath until the train had passed: besides I had medals for high diving, but not into a community of crocodiles. I counted the seconds - the engine was on me.

With a blundering rush and a mighty effort I threw the combination on to the bank and fell down beside it - SAVED! But imagine my mortification on seeing the train taking a siding a few yards before it reached the bridge.

I made Cape York next day but found the place uninteresting so I took the next ferry across the Torres Straits as I was overdue in Thursday Island.

23

A DUEL WITH SABRES ON THURSDAY ISLAND

While peacefully reclining in the lounge of The Royal Hotel in Thursday Island I noticed by my paper it was Friday 12th September 1924.

"Just fancy," I said aloud, "ten long years ago since I joined The Services in The Great War".

A Naval Officer from *HMS Herald* looked across and then joined me in a spot of whisky. We talked of many lands and peoples. We debated the point. He knew everything! I was a land lubber, I knew nothing! The debate became heated. Onlookers intervened. We were not satisfied. We agreed on one thing: we would settle it by combat. I offered fists, pistols, swords! It was midnight and our pals fixed up for 7 next morning, on Black Rock Beach.

We arrived on time determined to have 'satisfaction'. Sabres were placed in our hands and 1, 2, 3, we were off. We sparred and feinted, I was for getting on with the business and lunged for his shoulder. He side-stepped and winged me in the arm. Seeing my chance I quickly replied but he struck my sabre down and it entered his thigh. Our seconds called 'time'. Somehow we agreed that our honour had been vindicated and we had found 'satisfaction'. We gaily shook hands and cracked jokes while our wounds were being tended.

ARCHIBALD EDMUND FILBY

The Lieutenant and I became great pals and he fixed up for me to take a voyage with them all in *HMS Herald* (I was fourth officer) the English Survey Vessel. It was a grand trip. We steamed to Sydney and right round to Hong Kong, eventually returning to Thursday Island.

I prophesied that one of these days I would throw in my lot with the Navy . We had many a laugh over the little incident on 'The Black Rock of Thursday Island'.

[*HMS Herald* was originally launched in 1918 as *Merry Hampton*, a 24-class mine-sweeping sloop. In 1923 it was renamed *HMS Herald* and converted to a survey ship. She was scuttled in in 1942 at Singapore Naval Base, raised by the Japanese, renamed *Heiyo*, and sunk by a mine on 14 November 1944.]

24

BY SAILING LUGGER THROUGH THE PACIFIC

While sailing around Cape York I purchased a Japanese Pearling Lugger and it proved a cheap and serviceable boat, and, by the low price the Jap took for it I was pretty sure that it was not his to sell.

After doing fishing of all sorts in the Torres Straits, I took a most interesting voyage, quite leisurely through the Seas of Arafura, Banda, Flores and Java. I actually covered several months as I made many calls at islands on the way. On reaching Singapore I sold my lugger for five times the sum I gave for it.

Looking back at that marvellous little voyage, fraught with danger and surprises which lurked round every corner, I class it as one of the most enjoyable trips that I remember, especially as 'I paddled my own canoe' all the way. The description and photos of that bijou sail would make an educational and absorbing *Boys Own* Volume. Just run your finger along the course indicated and it will be observed that it passes through some of the wildest and picturesque Ocean scenery and Nationalities in the Orient.

In the course of the next two years I practically covered the whole of the North Pacific, the South Pacific Seas and continued right down and through the Southern Ocean and Indian Ocean. I voyaged in every conceivable craft including Mail Steamers, H.M. Survey Ships, Tugs, Speedboats, Luggers, Outriggers, Sampans, Canoes etc. At times I sailed from one island to another.

A Voyage of Exploration amongst the 3000 Pacific Islands with Headhunters and Cannibals.

Away up in the North Pacific Ocean we explored innumerable islands. The Solomons and the New Guinea Group cover very large areas, while others were so small that they did not seem to attract man of any kind. We usually ran into all sorts of weird humans, terrible looking chaps some of them! Many were sociable and tried to help, for they had had white visitors before and remembered that they got some nice little presents if they behaved themselves. Really they were like simple children for even they had to be watched carefully.

These natives would grunt and squeak to assist their gesticulations, while we shouted in various dialects, but it was only by signs and muscles that we could converse with them. Occasionally we came across a chap that knew a word or two, then we would take him along with us as a guide. Then, when he got the wind up and refused to proceed, we would load him with presents and start him back home. How the deuce he ever got there beat me, for the tracks were highly dangerous. I was told that they usually slept on a tree top for safety.

There is a popular notion that Cannibalism is a thing of the past. That however is not so! I had first-hand evidence of Cannibalism on many occasions. The natives of many islands are more than keen on a nice banquet of human flesh. I was never clear what their method or idea was in obtaining it. I do not think they would try to trap a missionary or traveller, neither did they resort to murder to satisfy their desire.

It appeared certain, however, that after a local battle they always produced rations for their local flesh pots to celebrate the fight, win or lose. Those were the nights of terrible orgies. They would continue to eat, drink and dance, cutting themselves with knives in their drunken madness, until they fainted with exhaustion and were thrown on one side. It was advisable to give them a wide berth on those nights of celebrations otherwise one might receive a much too cordial reception and appear on the bill of fare.

On the whole, however, these wild men seemed a fairly harmless set of animals, and one could live amongst them quite well for a spell at least. One thing in their favour was that they were not terribly afraid of a stranger like some tribes were. Those sort of gents will stalk one down and throw things at you such as arrows and rocks etc. I always had a good time with the natives but one must know how to treat them and quell any horseplay with no uncertain hand!

The study of the Wild man in his Homeland, is to me a joy.

25

A GLORIOUS EXPEDITION

Next, a Glorious Expedition through the Wilds of Papua New Guinea, The Friendlies, Polynesians and scores of other Pacific Islands.

One night after a boxing bout at the Drill Hall on Thursday Island, Harry Flannery introduced me to two hard-boiled world adventurers, both double my age, with the remark that this was just my chance! Pots of money, sacks of gold nuggets and untold marvels, etc. waiting to be picked up if you can persuade these gentlemen to take you with them. We all got to discussing a marvellous proposition and from data we acquired we were able to fix up financial agreements before the week was out.

We were to explore the the almost unmapped regions in the Gulf of Papua, Dutch New Guinea, Amboina, Banda, plus the islands around. There was always a great demand for tortoise shell, trocas shell, mother-of-pearl, birds of paradise, copra, oils and gums, gold and other precious metals, all of which were stated to be available in abundance in those regions mentioned.

We fitted out a motor boat and started away, calling at innumerable islands. The inhabitants of most of them were just wild men and quite unintelligent. In fact they refused to approach us, our motor boat, no doubt, adding to their terror.

At Port Moresby we filled up with petrol and other necessities. The Owen Stanley Range was an impressive sight. We eventually made Papua and then away to the Banda Sea calling at Ambon and Serain. We had a wonderful time with people of all nations such as Japanese, Chinese, Malayans and various natives of a very primitive order who might be an acquisition to a zoo but no use to us for our job of work. We made voyage to The Solomons, The Friendlies, The ... [at this point, this particular manuscript abruptly ends.]

I clearly recall my debut as a Pearl Diver.

Looking back over a quarter of a century of extensive foreign travel, it is of interest to note that the occurrences which gave me the most "kick" always seemed to have a humorous twist.

For instance I had just arrived on Thursday Island to meet a wartime [WW1] comrade of the late Royal Flying Corps [now the Royal Air Force] when I was introduced to Mr Walter Stevens, a huge fellow, the big gun of the Pearl Beds, of which he had full charge. Over a glass of the best in the T.I. [Thursday Island] Hotel, the conversation was all about the divers, the yield of pearls and the financial side of the business.

I began to feel that I was butting in, so I asked them to fill up their glasses, following that up by boldly asking them if it was possible for me to go down to the pearl beds in a diving suit tomorrow. Owing to a great silence and side looks, I felt that I had perhaps been hasty and had made a *faux pas*.

I walked around the room and noticed the front door was locked. I found it was only because the hotels there have to close at 6 pm. This is faithfully carried out but the back doors are thrown open until eight o'clock next morning.

I received a call to the bar so I felt I was forgiven. Not to be nonplussed, after spending the evening together, I thought the time right to repeat my question. I got Mr Stevens on one side and casually mentioned it.

"Oh, yes," replied Mr Stevens in a booming voice so that all the house could hear, "report at the landing stage at 10 o'clock tomorrow."

That night the conversation was about pearls and diving. One rough looking diver kept murmuring away about, "...that young Scotch chap who would go down to look at the oysters. I felt sorry for the parson having to break the bad news to his gal. But those life-lines will tangle! Poor chap."

I got excited about the stories of fish as big as ponies which attack on sight. There were a dozen awkward stories about trouble with life-lines.

One man said to me, "If ever you go down, never drink the night before, always brings on heart failure!"

At 10 o'clock I was there and we were soon over the spot to descend. Many willing hands put me into the cumbersome diving suite, with only the helmet to screw on.

Last words before going: "There is a school of savage barracuda about today, they are sure to attack you." I was then handed a huge knife which had a hilt each end. "Now don't go trying to stab them, they're much too fast. Just hold up the knife and the fish will go for the flash of the steel. As it closes its mouth the blade will go right through its jaw. You let go and signal and we will haul you up. Should you see a shark, that's different. There are some nasty fellows about. Just put your fingers in between your wrist band and suit and the flow of bubbles will soon frighten those chaps away."

All these instructions did not reassure me, a novice, and the screwing on of the helmet was, for me, not a jolly process which it might be to others. Plenty of hands helped me over the side of the boat and my gigantic weighted boots were guided onto the first rung of the ladder. It was not encouraging to see the casual way the boys were working the air pumps: making cigarettes with their hands and kicking the pump handles with their toes. I would have liked to sack them on the spot.

Feeling my way clumsily down the ladder, the water rushed over me. Before I was completely submerged, there was a frightful crash which completely unnerved me. This was followed by a jerk and a dead stop.

Ye Gods! What do I do next? Of course! The life-lines had fouled! I threw myself backwards with a mighty effort so I could look up through my window. In so doing I dislodged my mighty breastplate from the rungs of the ladder which had been the cause of the sudden stop. Then, losing my hold, I sank rapidly to the bottom. (I later discovered that the crash I had experienced was caused by one of the crowd who tapped my helmet with a piece of wood.)

Now on the bed of the ocean my first look chanced upon what appeared to be a huge vertebrate animal coming for me. Grabbing desperately for my knife I promptly dropped it. Next move was to push my fingers my wrist band and I was rewarded with a wonderful display of bubbles.

I immediately became aware of blood pressure and being scared I quickly closed the vent. The whole suit consequently blew out to its fullest extent causing me to rush to the surface with my legs and arms fully extended. I was then grabbed by the gang and hauled in, life-lines and all, in the most inglorious fashion, amid the boisterous mirth of my tormentors.

My next address was Galle Face Hotel, Columbo. Then a long run through India, China, Japan, Korea, etc. which took up several years.

26

THREE MONTHS ON THE ISLAND OF CEYLON

I spent three months on the Island of Ceylon [Sri Lanka]. This land of the Cingalese (area 25,000 square miles) has its own defence force.

Whenever I visit that beautiful sweetly scented tropical island I always make straight for The Galle Face Hotel in Columbo. What an hotel! Actually it is more like a palace than an hotel. The dining room seats 2,000 with ease and the food and service is excellent. The lounge, or one of them, holds even more.

The ornate and up-to-date baths are a feature. The swimming pool and diving lagoon has water changed at every tide. The gardens and grounds contain sufficient tropical fruits and flowers to make it rank as one of the finest shows imaginable.

On one occasion I was with a hunting party that put up with the Mount Lavinia Grand Hotel just outside Mount Lavinia not far from Columbo. A more picturesque and sociable place would be almost impossible to find.

This time on my arrival I was met at the quay by by some old chums who were tea planters on a big scale on the island. We all went over to the Galle Face for tiffin and I booked a suite of chambers for three months.

My friends insisted upon me going down to their estate at Kandy to fulfil my promise of five years ago, their wives and families were expecting me at once.

"Well," I said, "if business interferes with pleasure, I suppose I must give up business."

They helped me pack a bag and away we went across to Kandy.

I don't know how many days we spent together but I do know we had a really glorious time. Driving scores of miles through the beautiful country on good roads, taking part in shoots of big game and small game, I acquired enough trophies to stock a museum. Sad to relate I never got anything of my collection home at all.

For two days we toured the hills and mountains of the Piduratalaga over 8,000 feet up, picnicking and fishing. I only escaped from the kind clutches of my hosts when we called in the hotel for a drink. I threatened them with a gun, that if they did not clear out and leave me to get on with my programme I should have to make trophies of them.

I engaged a good secretary to help me cope with the arrears of work. Of course, I was representing a motor firm. I expected big business and I was not disappointed.

The three months slid away like weeks. I gathered together my trunks and baggage (and quite a lot of the portable trophies) for one lady offered me a stuffed elephant on wheels which I graciously declined on the grounds that it might startle my parents.

I sailed away to Singapore, a run of almost 1,500 miles, where I anticipated making agreements, to cover India and The Far East, for the next few years.

27

BORNEO AND SARAWAK

Just a word or two about this beautiful and up-to-date island. From Batavia [present day Jakarta] I crossed the Java Sea to Borneo landing at Pontianak on the River Kapuas.

On my motor cycle I proceeded North somewhat leisurely calling at the little towns on the way. Sambas and Kuching both provided good refreshment and a rest.

The next day I passed through Sarawak, visiting some business people at Bintulu. I received a most cordial welcome from these polished courteous people who pressed me to stay as long as I liked with them. As I was already many months in arrears with my programme I regretfully decided to carry on to British North Borneo.

I made the town of Jesselton [Kota Kinabalu] my quarters, a place of neat streets and pretty buildings. Here I made many friends who initiated me into their clubs. We had some glorious times. The picnic we had up the Kinabalu Volcano will leave pleasant memories with me for all time.

The island appears to be a large place, with its 1,000 miles by 600 and is situated right on the line of the Equator. I was much struck with the superior class of the people and their friendliness.

I really could not prolong my stay any further as I wished to be in

Singapore very soon. I gave a farewell night to my Borneo pals and motored down to Baram Point, Sarawak, then shipped to Sumatra.

I promised the 'Borneonians' that when I settled down in life, perchance in smoky old London suburbs, I would have my country house in beautiful tropical Borneo.

28

JAVA

Another trip which proved most pleasurable and remunerative was from Batavia [now Central Jakarta] in Dutch East Indies [Indonesia], to Surabaya in Java. At the N.V. Orange Hotel in Surabaya, I fell in with two Birmingham lads and we all set off on motor cycles to do the Island.

The scenery was beautiful in the extreme all the way. The volcanoes were very fascinating and we explored several of the largest. We climbed Mount Bromo by rushing our machines up in short stages, much to the interest of the natives, who rushed around apparently expecting to pick up any pieces we might have dropped.

At 6,300 feet we stopped the night and the next day we resumed our ascent on some fine sturdy Java ponies which we rode, pulled and helped scramble to the top. By crawling on our stomachs and lying flat we could peer over the top of the crater. At intervals the wind would clear the belching smoke and steam so that we could clutch on the lip and see right down into the volcano basin. Continuous rumblings and explosions were going on all the time, which was rather unnerving, as we expected an upheaval at any moment. The noise seemed like umpteen railway trains rushing through an iron tunnel. We took some good photos and were not sorry to go back to the comfort of our hotel again that night.

The foregoing pages record just a brief outline of my travels and adventures in those great free and unspoiled countries of the Continent of Asia and neighbouring lands. I can honestly say I had some of the most exciting and pleasurable times of my life. Remember I was only 23 years old then and I said, "All's right with the world."

At Surabaya I was introduced to Jack Gregson of Dunlop Limited and also Mr Bert Cathrick in an allied trade. Together we motored and picnicked the whole Island.

The Island of Java is about 700 miles long and 60 miles wide. Of course it is a Dutch possession but British appears to predominate especially as far as status is concerned. For instance I was made a member of the Swagger Club there and on my second visit I said to the Steward, "Oh! You might let me have a pound or two, just over the weekend, as we are going picnicking up the Sermiti."

"Certainly, Sir, how much do you require?"

But one day I heard a prosperous looking Dutch member say, "George, can you oblige me with a little cash till tomorrow?"

"Sorry, oh sorry, Sir, I dare not do it!" ejaculated the Steward, bowing and scraping, "Against all the rules, Sir!"

As a matter of fact the Steward was also Dutch.

A slight diversion - In the Dutch East Indies [Indonesia] I give my expert services to help raid an opium den.

Yes, I was just the man they wanted for the job. So with visions of some fun or bloodshed, I was to go on in advance. My role was to go as a smoking client and get the general lay of the land and when they signalled I was to see they got in even if I had to knock out the Chinese owners or attendants. As an ordinary white man or tourist I should not be suspected!

All went according to plan, I gave out tips lavishly and received overwhelming attention from the Natives who knew their business. They quietly padded around, kept my pipe filled and bolstered me up with cushions. I must have lost all thought of detective work as I drifted away into joyous dreams. I had a feeling that fights and quarrels were going on but that was only just a normal phase.

Now the unfortunate part of the whole affair was that I had entered the wrong house! Our raiding party met serious opposition and searched for me in vain. The raid was a complete failure. My share for the next two days was a continuous bullying of which I took no notice as my splitting headache from the narcotic of the white poppy kept me fully engaged.

On the third day I was able to sit up and take notice and I lost no time in informing my dear pals exactly what I thought of THEM!

With the assistance of some official guides we spent two days exploring the Bromo Mountains, the volcanic craters, which extend many acres, and the caves where the famous prehistoric remains were found that is The Ape Man of Java dated 5,000 years B.C.

Some of the roads of Java are quite good as they wind through difficult country and mountain passes, showing clever engineering. For many miles we followed the railway, with the little puffing billy running alongside, then as we drew away from it, it would catch us up again when we stopped in the towns much to the huge delight of the passengers.

We also did a lot of horseback riding on the native sturdy hill ponies, each accompanied with a mounted and very capable groom. These Javanese fellows were very strong and sinewy, with bare feet, small appetites and life teetotallers.

It was in the Dutch East Indies [Indonesia] that I first came in touch with John Castley, Editorial Representative of The Motor Cycle, Tudor Street, London. His colleague, Bert Cathrick, and he were on a World Tour for B.S.A. Birmingham. Both were riding motor cycle combinations. I purchased a similar one but I usually stuck to my car.

We were of great mutual assistance during our happy association. Their itinerary embraced London, France, Portugal, Spain, Italy, Austria, Czechoslovakia, Hungary, Jugoslavia, Bulgaria, Turkey, Asia

Minor, Syria, Palestine, Sinai Desert, Egypt, India, China, Japan, Malay States, Australia and then on and on. With promises of reunion in other countries I left them in Java.

I have very pleasant reminiscences of my stay on the beautiful island of Java. When the time came for leaving, they gave me a right royal send off. With the British Consul in the Chair, I was the guest of honour. Many business heads supported the function. I thanked them all for the many kindnesses I had received at their hands but really must wish them adieu as I had appointments in British North Borneo. That was in 1925.

Subsequently I proceeded to the Province of Sarawak, embarking from Baram Point to Sumatra, landing at Lampong. Then on to Jambi, all the while with my car. I did good business in the Federated Malay States and was appointed Sales Manager to Malayan Motors Limited, with Headquarters at Singapore.

29

ORIENTAL WAYS

It's a very lazy life here in the Far East for a European. It is almost unknown for a 'white' to do menial or manual work. One does so little for one's self. Servants, or boys, as they are often called, hover around by the dozen, all fussing to do their bit for the great Sahib. One takes off my shoes, another slips on my slippers. Two boys bring in trays of drinks and scrape around pouring them out. They will stand holding the glass out until their arm aches or you take the drink from them. More boys with pipes, cigarettes and matches which are lighted and burnt out long before required. Another keeps me fanned, another rocks my chair by request, unceasingly for an hour. One holds my book at an angle for me to read and so on and so *ad libitum*.

Suddenly I wave my arms and yell, "Clear out, every one of you!" perhaps in somewhat coarse language and in Malayan, and away they fly leaving me in peace. No wonder that I find I am rapidly putting on weight.

Now from our lounge we observe a body of Priests ceremoniously bathing their sacred bull on the silvery sea shore. It strikes us as being so ridiculous, their chantings and offerings, that I suggest chucking something at them. Anyway, I'm afraid that we made great fun of it all, of course clandestinely, otherwise there may have been fearful trouble with their followers.

We paid a visit one day to a Buddhist Temple, and by anointing the Priests palms with a few rupees, we were allowed the privilege of seeing The Tooth of Buddha in the 2,000 year old Temple of The Tooth.

※

During one of my calls at Singapore, I recall a stirring encounter. I availed myself of an invitation from an old friend, Jimmy 'A'. Jimmy and I had much in common and conversation flowed freely. A few friends had looked in and over a few yarns, chiefly of travel, I heard of some methods 'the Dick Turpins of the Road' were busy working.

I was keenly interested in all this as I had been waylaid and held up by some 'gentlemen of the road' when coming through Srivilliputhur, in the Punjab. On that awkward occasion I only got away by strategy and by the fact of having a high power car.

The present scheme, however, appeared to be an ambush set on a main road at some quiet spot. One of them would lie in the road as though injured and the unsuspecting motorist would stop and get out to investigate. That was the immediate signal to let drive with their shot guns and ask questions, if necessary, later.

One night, shortly after this conversation, I was returning from Kota Bharu with Jimmy and two ladies in the car and we again got onto the same subject as we had heard of more exploits of the outlaws. We were very sorry to find that our lady friends had become unnerved through our talking so much about it.

Just here the road was running practically on the foreshore, the phosphorescent waves were almost lapping the road, the huge palms (some of the tallest in the world) nodded to and fro in the gentle midnight breeze. The full moon bathed all in a weird white light, producing quite an uncanny setting while the thuds of the surf beat a ceaseless muffled rhythm with the throb of our engine. To give my fair passengers the best effect of this weird and beautiful scene, I turned the car on a little loop road.

My ears were immediately assailed by the piercing shrieks from the ladies, followed by an urgent command from Jimmy to GO LIKE HELL. I ceased admiring the moon and saw, 25 yards in front of us, a real live Buddha sitting almost in the middle of the narrow track, swaying backwards and forwards. Too late to turn back, no doubt we were being ambushed, it was a trick of the bandits.

I took Jimmy's advice and jammed on the accelerator and rushed past the rocking giant, mentally deciding to leave him alone, although my car almost caught him.

The ladies automatically slid off the back seats to the floor, as there they were far less likely to be hit by flying bullets, while Jimmy gingerly cast a wary eye around. He observed that the old man was sticking his ground where he was.

Although we were in grave doubt about it all, we maintained a high speed right up to our hotel in Singapore, where we broadcast the news to an excited audience.

After dropping off the ladies and seeing they had a pick-me-up, in which we courteously joined, we decided on a course of action to double-cross the bandits. Several sportsmen, just returned from a shoot, were all for crowding into the car with us, and so off we went to have a pot shot at these Chinese highwaymen.

We allowed two to join us and, all armed, we pushed off again in record time amid the cheers of our friends. I noticed a commotion amongst them and guessed that many of them would follow on. We might be glad of reinforcements should we find ourselves outnumbered or cornered.

Our plan was to carefully approach the spot where we had seen the decoy, stop and pretend to get out. Of course we would have our guns trained on the bank opposite the sea. Beyond that we could not plan but wait and see what happened and then accommodate them.

Yes, there he was and bigger than ever he looked. How he shone! We were right on him now. Our decoy man is now on the running board and I have nearly stopped but am cautiously moving along.

Our decoy man can't stand the tension and is almost touching this weird giant who seems oblivious of the world. Our man lets go a terrific yell and leaps off the car at the Buddha. Goodness, is our man shot, electrocuted or what? No, he seems alright, but the huge Chinaman is up and shambling away into the woods. He is completely nude and shines like a piece of bronze as he is anointed with oil from head to foot.

What are we going to do about it?

Two of our party get out and reconnoitre, with their fingers on the triggers of their revolvers, walking up and down, asking for trouble. Still nothing doing. We ease up and have a smoke and pass the flask around. We stroll down to the shore.

Hark! What a din! Fools! We are quite unprepared now. Had we laughed too soon? Several Malayans and Chinese are rushing at us. We're trapped! But... What are they yelling?

"Don'tee drownee poo Billee Li Lo Chang! Don'tee shootee him!"

We then noticed several cars up on the road discharging their crews and recognised some of our friends from the hotel running towards us in the dim light. They were roaring with laughter.

They explained that when the kitchen boys heard about the Buddha which had altered our course, four of them had asked to be taken along to explain what was happening.

The boys said, "Why, sir that is only poo oldee Billee Li Lo Chang! He's gentleman, no robber. Save him from Sahib's guns!"

It appears that he was a well-known character in the place and quite a favourite among the local Malayans. His wife had been thrown off and killed from a cart he was driving at that spot by the seaside. Now at every full moon he would anoint himself with oil and hold a vigil while waiting for the return of his lost wife.

30

MORE PEARL DIVING AND I VISIT BALI

Once again a little trip by water landed me at Singapore, always a favourite spot of mine. The temperature there is always equable, ranging around 86°F (30°C) all the year round.

In January, 1926, I was writing up my diary during some quiet moments on board The China Navigation Company Steam Ship *Tiayuian*. I had taken a fine collection of photos during my jaunt to Thursday Island.

It was there I fell in with the bosses of the Pearling Fleet. They agreed to let me go down and look at the oyster beds and down I went again in a diving suit. It was a strange experience, but better than my first attempt and I greatly preferred it to groping my way in the deep gold mines in Johannesburg or perhaps the nerve racking adventures of exploration I had in Australia's Mammoth Caves where one slip and not a shred of evidence would be left to tell the tale.

I was loath to leave my pearling friends who had given me a really good time. I then accepted an invitation from an officer on His Majesty's Ship *Herald* to spend a week with them as guest. This vessel was on a government survey and I was initiated into some of its mysteries. It certainly was most interesting work and I was offered a post with them but I turned it down and and sailed away to New Guinea.

There I made some pals and fixed up a trek up country to Papua, about 400 miles through trackless country. We had a lot of bother with the native carriers. It was actually impossible to do any business with them. They are just savages of very low intelligence, and still cannibals, so we anticipated a spot of fun.

We made some sort of headway for two days but on the third morning we found that half of our black mob had stampeded home again. They were a senseless lot entirely without the faculty of thinking. That put an end to our trek and we returned with much difficulty to Daru again. After a couple of weeks of roaming New Guinea, I cut across through Thursday Island to Carmo. Dr Jessop of Straits Settlement had kindly offered to take my correspondence for a time while I travelled in China and Japan.

It was August 1926 when I took appointment of Head Salesman for Straits Settlement Motor Company and I opened up at the Sea View Hotel, Tangjong, Kalong, Singapore, a really wonderful hotel with grounds reaching down to the sea. Between times we had a lot of sport, riding and hunting in the jungle and on the rubber estates. Before returning to my Headquarters at Singapore we visited the Famous Spice-Scented Isle of Bali.

Bali (one of the Dutch East Indies Sunda Island Group) is just a short run across the channel from Banyuwang, Java. Our boat was pulled up on the beach by energetic fishermen and a charming Balinese lady officially welcomed us. A waiting carriage carried us up the coral and teak pave to our hotel.

Visitors are always welcomed as they are the mainstay of the Island's business. The Balinese are however a most industrious race, producing sufficient food to meet their needs. They make innumerable souvenirs, such as paintings, statues, pictures and models of the world's renowned Balinese dancers. Few ever leave the island, which has often been described as a Natural Paradise. The Islanders have 30 gods, no unions or politics, and live a simple, happy life.

Young ladies came from a thousand village temples whose bells are incessantly ringing. We selected the chief theatres and admired their talents. The young ladies were mostly of marriageable age, between (and including) 13 to 16. We were rather amazed at the casualness of the young women, entirely unclothed as they, together with other villagers, rollicked in the rolling surf under a blazing sun.

The dancing girls looked lovely in their magnificent ceremonial dresses. They seemed to have non-stop programmes, including feasts and parades, led by a prima ballerina, usually a daughter of a Rajah. The dances were a wonderful feature but I thought their shows were over-long. Perhaps they were used to too much leisure in their villages under the everlasting tropical sky. Their weird orchestra, or gamelan of drums, gongs, xylophones, etc. decorated with red, silver and gold, made the conglomeration of princesses, dragons and witches into fascinating entertainment. A Balinese male gave a dance based on the bumblebee and another, called Kebiar, was cleverly performed in a squatting position.

Their foods are very simple, just dried spiced lamb, rice and vegetables. They consume much plain tea, drink no wine and soft drinks are courteously refused as being too strong.

31

TIGER! TIGER!

Although I had been in the Federated Malay States for some time, I had not the opportunity of shooting a tiger and greatly coveted the chance to bag one. So when the manager of a rubber estate in Jahore invited me to stay with him, I accepted with alacrity as tigers were frequently met with there and my host was known to be a most successful tiger hunter.

Life on a rubber plantation is pretty much a routine affair and the first few days of my stay were pleasant but uneventful and as much alike as the slender rubber trees that stretched away in endless straight row after straight row.

Then came the exciting news that a tiger had been seen round the native quarters and my host and I set out to shoot it. My enthusiasm was somewhat dampened, however, by my first sight of his gun, an antiquated affair of huge calibre whose barrel was fastened to the stock with baling wire. We did not meet the tiger that night, for which I was devoutly thankful, as I would rather have faced him without a weapon than have fired the thing.

Another guest was expected, a junior officer from India, who was also reported to be a very keen hunter. When he arrived in a car completely equipped for the chase and unloaded his kit, we found that he possessed the most up to date armoury that money could buy.

Almost his first words were, "How soon can I get a tiger, d'you think?" so arrangements were made for the following night. He supervised a suitable tree in which to build a shooting platform, somewhat to the mystification of my friend, who, as far as I could make out, simply walked out casually and shot tigers.

The conversation naturally turned on guns and we were treated to a selection of some of the finest examples of the gunsmith's art. Our new guest was rather caustic about my friend's cannon, and kindly offered to lend us one of his beauties.

The following evening at the appointed hour, one of the native boys brought the goat which was to serve as bait, and we set off dragging the unwilling brute after us on a rope. Slung round our shoulders were special airtight containers full of sandwiches and flasks of ready-mixed whisky and soda. We were also carrying rugs and cushions, to the great amusement of my friend and the boys.

Long before our destination we were warned to move very quietly, an instruction that the goat unfortunately didn't understand, for with a loud "Maaaa-aa-a" it ran round the wrong side of a tree, hopelessly entangling itself and its leader in the rope.

There was no doubt that our guest was keen and was out to show that he was willing to do his fair share of the work, for without hesitation he picked up the animal and staggered on with it clutched in his arms. This and the darkness prevented him from seeing the many roots that snaked across the path and as we neared our tree he stumbled over one of these and went crashing down.

As he fell there was a terrific report and my host and I, thinking one of his guns had gone off, instinctively ducked for cover. He sat up, however, still firmly holding the goat on his lap and said, "Sorry, old boy, but I'm afraid one of our whisky flasks has burst."

With subdued chuckles we followed him until we reached the hideout, when he set about placing small white stones at varying distances from the trunk, "so that you can get the range when it's dark, you know."

The goat was then tethered to a stump and we were all ready. Climbing the tree laden as we were with equipment was not easy and what with the general scuffling and the breaking of branches my friend said he would eat his hat if there was a tiger within miles.

Spreading out the rugs and cushions on the platform, we settled ourselves to wait. Time passed. Our host fell asleep, began to snore loudly and had to be wakened. The goat had also gone to sleep. It was suggested that unless it bleated or baaed, whichever a goat does, the tiger wouldn't know it was there. I offered to go down and stir it up but our guest pointed out that this was dangerous work as the tiger might be close at hand. It would therefore be only sporting if we drew lots to see who should go. Three twigs of different lengths were broken off and our guest drew the longest.

With exaggerated caution he began to descend. As soon as his head was below the level of the platform my friend and I basely began to tuck into the sandwiches and remaining flask. Having done so, my friend leaned over the edge of the platform and hissed, "Here he comes!" causing our guest to scramble up the tree at terrific speed.

There was another long wait, through which the goat slumbered peacefully, and presently down he went again, but there was no sign of Stripes. The discovery that all the sandwiches had been eaten seemed to dampen our guest's ardour so we decided to go home and try again another night.

The goat seemed highly relieved to find that it was being taken home but gave further trouble with its rope on the way and we were all badly scared by a wild boar that dashed across our path. However we arrived back safely, bade the enthusiastic sportsman good night at the entrance of the small hut he was occupying some twenty yards distant from the main house and were soon in bed and asleep.

In the early hours of the morning my dreams were shattered by wild yells of, "Tiger, tiger!" I dashed frantically out to the hut to find my host already there and a very sheepish looking guest sitting up in bed, but no tiger. The joke was definitely on him and I must say he took it in good part. He had been dreaming of tigers, he explained, when he had suddenly become aware of movement on his pillow. Still half asleep, he had put up his hand, and to his horror, touched - fur! Our host's cat had brought her kittens into the hut and carefully placed them on his bed for warmth.

32

MOTOR BUSINESS IN THE FAR EAST

In January 1927 I took up my appointment as Chief Factory Representative of The New Hadfield Bean Cars Company Limited, an all British firm.

The fine modern factory at Tipton, Birmingham, was replete with every modern appliance to make our cars a first class job. The showrooms at 11 Regent Street, London, was a rendezvous for automobile connoisseurs from all lands. The whole being under the business eye of Lord Hadfield, whose famous Sheffield Steels were embodied in the Bean cars.

My area covered the whole of the Near and Far East, with my headquarters and offices at Battery Road, Singapore. One advantage of fixing my domicile and centre there was I was not subject to British Income Tax, a great consideration as my salary and allowances were in the vicinity of £3,000 per annum.

I was not running on a commission basis although I must have sold many scores of cars. My position was to fix up responsible and influential agencies in the Chief Centres of The East and to see that the business was conducted along the right lines. It was impressed upon me that all my actions and dealings were to be first class. That applied to hotels, special trains, aeroplanes, horses, liners or any other transport. Last, but not least, the class and position of the people I came in contact with. Money was a secondary consideration. I very soon realised that this advice was most sound. Impressions and self valuation go a long way in the East, even more so than the West.

I had absolutely full power to act on behalf of the company. I floated two new companies for the Bean car, one in Singapore and the other in Madras. I found it rather a ticklish job but I was able to procure good legal and business advice and the companies were successfully floated.

I had my own six cylinder Hadfield Bean 14/70 Sports Car (no saloon for me, whatever the weather). This car could accelerate to 70 miles per hour in less than half a minute with no vibration whatever, taking stiff gradients at over 50 mph. Above all one could drive at any speed with security knowing the vital parts are made from reliable Hadfield steel. I also had the call upon as many of our cars as I wished at any time or place.

Many thousands of miles were done on liners and some tiresome journeys were negotiated by aeroplane. I made my own running, travelling from one country to another as my ideas or fortune indicated. One will note in the following descriptions of my peregrinations that they were here, there, back and forward, much as a London Commercial might do.

I started right away through the Federated Malay States, putting up in Penang at the Runnymede Hotel. Then across to Johore and Malaya, on to China, Japan, Korea, right across the vast states of India, taking in Burma, up the Irrawaddy River to Mandalay. It was November when I left Madras taking a run to Pondicherry and Bangkok.

Combining pleasure with business, for too much of the latter is not popular in the East, I joined some splendid outings and was able to accept many invitations for yachting, mountaineering, big-game hunting, and social and business gatherings.

The big-game hunts up country were the most thrilling, stalking and trapping tiger, elephant and lesser denizens of the jungle. The hunt outfit comprised as many as 50 people, each with his separate duties. The excitement of everybody, including the old hands at these kills, was beyond description. Our lives were often in jeopardy - just touch and go! – but our parties came through safely with the exception of few minor accidents and some bad scares.

It was a new one on me when I was invited to a Dutch Hotel, The Van Wiegt, with a notable party of huntsmen. There was a mixed but well-to-do crowd there, consisting of Danes, Germans, Italians, French, and a preponderance of Dutchmen. The way tiffin was put on was wonderful. Go East if you want to taste the glorious curry that only their chefs can produce! Does rice trifle sound simple? This is where a novice chef will fail without a helpful pal to coach him.

A very large empty plate commences the function, (for it is more than a meal) then over 30 dishes are brought along by the waiters, or boys as we call them. Each one bears a separate variety which goes to make up a complete meal or tiffin. It would appear to be discourteous should you decline to take a little from each dish.

At the end of this Dutch tiffin, which has taken well over two hours, and of course accompanied by choice wines and liqueurs, we all felt as though a twenty-four hour rest was needed. Anyway, it's a glorious experience if taken in the right company.

The travel continued through the Malay States. The population is chiefly Chinese and Malay. The natives are full of superstition: the boats have eyes to see where they are going, the houses have ears to pick up news or scandal for their owners, the doors have noses to scent good or evil entering, the carts have feet for transport and so on. The ideas are made the most of and acted upon.

The temperature remains around 80°F [27°C] and when it rains, which is seldom, it flops down as though cisterns are being turned upside down and seldom gives one time to rush for shelter.

The better class of Chinese have much more money than sense to use it. All Chinese seem ludicrous in their cash dealings. They usually pay or ask too much or too little. Death means nothing to these stolid gentry. They appear to be without fear in that direction and commit hari kari apparently for the love of the thing.

A funeral is often a showy affair. I observed a Chinaman starting off the opposite way the cortege was going. He was playing a sort of bagpipes, throwing imitation bank notes in to the air, pausing to have a little bonfire with more notes, then chanting to his god to protect the soul of the deceased. All this was to decoy the devil away from the resting place of the departed.

I next made a call at Jahore where I was the honoured guest of The Sultan himself. He surely did me well, money was tipped out like water and I certainly had a royal time. He asked me to supply him with a variety of motor chariots and circus processional cars to hold some of his retinue. He wanted big running boards and shelves placed at conspicuous angles to prop them on. He told me he was not going to take second place to those damned Princes in neighbouring states. Anyway he had the good sense to order some of our best Bean cars for his own use.

He was a brainy old boy and liked to have a bit of fun. While chatting in his palace about many serious world problems, I noticed a large number of his native people doing obeisance to His Majesty before the open doors. He nodded to the attendants to again charge our glasses and I followed his example of instantly emptying them. Then he touched my arm and made a few passes over the crowd on their knees in front of him. That drew their special attention. Next he gave forth a series of deep bellows, or groans, accompanied by the most fearful grimaces which would have put any comedian in the shade.

What happened? Why the worshippers took to their heels and raced away screaming with fear, joined by all in the vicinity. Both The Sultan and I rolled over with laughter at this extraordinary scene.

Another great potentate who gave me a most marvellous time would always go so far in his cups. I well remember after a hectic day we were having a restful evening with a few callers. Yarns from many lands were told and twice told. We swore eternal friendship many times over. I noticed the early morning workers starting out and I thought I would go while the going was good. This Ruler gave me to understand that I could not go like that and not trusting his legs he instructed his retinue to hand him several things. Taking a huge gold cigar case he folded a wad of bank notes and crammed them into it. He then pressed the beautiful gold case upon me, refusing to listen to my protests of refusal and thanks.

Early the following evening I called upon him and received a hearty reception. I replied by slapping this distinguished personage on his massive back, saying, "You're a damned old fool! Can't you look after your money better than that?" then I slipped his valuable golden case, crammed with rupees, into the folds of his silver tunic. I pretended to be very annoyed and said gruffly, "And look after it next time."

The old Sultan seemed so upset at my unkind attitude that he looked like bursting into tears as I jumped into my waiting car and shouted goodbye.

Now I have a confession to make. Of course money means so little to these potentates. It comes so easily. Just a little more tax on their subjects and in it rolls. Yes, I will confess that during my later travels I have remembered and regretted (maybe) my generous act of giving back that golden gift.

Down Southern India, through the State of Madras, I drove into the city at 4pm and noticed that the central clock indicated that it was precisely 10:45am in London. Here I struck quite a language difficulty, more especially with the workmen or artisans. I found that Tamil was about the only language taught in the schools.

The native vendors and bazaar kiosk keepers were a curious nondescript crowd of traders. Many of them went about their business almost naked, save a strip of loincloth while others were absurdly over dressed with English coats and waistcoats, usually four sizes too large for them. Their legs were encased in huge baggy trousers which flopped around them like flowing skirts. On their heads they seemed to balance outsized turbans. These last mentioned gentlemen were mostly Pathans who had come in from the North.

In the accompanying photograph, my Bean Tourer is shown on the run from the Union of of The Soviet Republic frontier, down South through Afghanistan, Beluchistan and Sind.

I discovered that the native chiefs (the majority of whom were opulent) as well as the rank and file had a great bump for pomp and show and were all curious to be in the know if anything out of the ordinary was doing. So my up-to-date car caused great excitement amongst them.

With that fact in my mind and on reaching Kabul I placed a notice board on each side of the car announcing some of the towns I was calling at en route to Bombay. This had an immediate effect. I was much more than an ordinary traveller and the car became a wonder.

I was escorted before the potentates and chief business men as soon as the news of my movements became known. This did have its drawbacks as many of them insisted on feting me and seemed to think that I should stay with them for ever instead of spending just a day or two in their palatial palaces.

It was a big pull up the Khyber Pass with a fair road and a steep drop in to Pershawar, then on to Dera Ismail Khan. In Kandahar I fixed up an agency, covering many thousands of miles, with the Principal of the National Garages, an influential firm with many branches. The town of Chamin, which I had put on my list, proved to be only just an interesting native village.

The garrison town of Quetta, quite a large military station, gave me a hearty welcome and of course so home-like was it that I felt I might really be in Aldershot or Woolwich. I was bombarded with questions such as: what was the latest from London; what was the Prime Minister going to do about this, that and the other; is the Air Ministry taking immediate steps, etc. etc. Of course I gave them secret and reliable information, it being several years since I had left England! I have to thank Colonel Galloway of the 109th Ghurkha Rifles who saw to it that I thoroughly enjoyed my visit there.

Crossing the Indus I made for Lahore and stayed at the Fallettes Hotel for 28 days. On again to the cool hills of Rawalpindi, my address being Flashmans Hotel. I soon discovered two or three Wartime colleagues of the Queen's Own Royal West Kent Rifles. These had decided to make the Army their profession and they certainly looked well and happy in it. I spent many pleasant hours with the officers of the British Garrison on this important Northwest Frontier Station. Their job was no sinecure and they were always on the alert. Surprises and skirmishes with the neighbouring turbulent tribes was not infrequent.

Next Patrala Saharanpux. My best connection there was Dr Ralan Rawlley, Director of Labour and Industries Bureau. I subsequently spent a few days in Kashmir Province, the Cecil Hotel, Murree was my temporary offices and reception rooms. Just seven days each at

Corstorphans Hotel and Fallettis Cecil Hotel, then away across the Ganges.

I ran into the City of Delhi, or shall I say Cities? There seemed to be half a dozen of them. Each time I pulled up and enquired for a place it was always, "Ah, Sir! It's in the other Delhi about five miles further on, etc. etc." Anyhow I sorted out New Delhi and took chambers at the Maidens Hotel where I stayed several months and covered the outlaying districts. I was able to arrange valuable contracts with Mr de Mello, the Secretary of the Transport Company, and Mr Nathaniel Orde of the Automobile Company.

During my stay in New Delhi I twice represented my firm at the Princes Conferences and also at other Public Functions. The Princes and Potentates would order Bean Cars off me (cash down) as casually as one would order a suit or two, when they took their fancy. Big business will undoubtedly accrue if my appointed agents can make delivery. I had to cable urgently to Mr Noel Martin, Managing Director of Bean Cars, Tipton, England. I regret that there was a great delay in delivering the cars although the money was waiting.

Lucknow was my next important stop. Here I appointed The Pioneer Motor Engineering Works at Abbotts Road as agents. Then away to Cawnpore [Kanpur], Benares and away down the Hooghly River to Calcutta putting up at the Great Eastern Hotel. That journey took several months.

At Calcutta I made arrangements with Mr Earnest Park of the Dunlop Tyre and Rubber Company and Mr Charles Lancaster who represented the Austin and Essex cars. I well remember the many outings with Mr Billy Moylan who took me under his wing and introduced me to all that was worth knowing. He saved me bags of trouble to say nothing of expense. For instance he kindly arranged that my car was ready in the morning and waiting in his show rooms. This was a great convenience to me as skilled labour was never prolific in those parts. I could write many chapters on Calcutta with its curious native sights, its wonderful mosques, temples and gorgeous hotels.

Other contracts were made with Mr Arthur Cutler, Manager of Goodyear Tyre and Rubber Company and also Mr Andrew Wilson of Stewart and Lloyds, Glasgow. Remembering I had received many and various pressing invites from my old friend, Mr Charles Caldero, who was now Editor of the Rangoon Times and Imperial Motors, I decided to travel to Madras and look him up.

About the first person I saw on entering the main street of Madras was Charley. To say he was surprised at being hailed by me would be putting it mildly. Away we went to his charming house where his wife and family received me with open arms and I will say they made my visit a memorable one.

Later I took a run to Pondicherry. This proved to be a good social and business centre. I had an introduction to Mr Leon Steed of Goodyear Tyre fame. I also arranged with Mr Nawabapitiya Gordon at Hoshangabad.

I then took a hop by aeroplane to the West Coast calling at principal towns down to Mysore where I fixed up a lot of business. Back once again inland to Bangalore where I made Lavenders Hotel my headquarters for several months.

Bangalore has a large European colony and we had many a merry time at Jimmy Lavenders during my extended visit and I made lots of useful friends. The silver tankard that was presented to me 'for valour' with much ceremony on my departure, and the many happy reminiscences, will long be treasured by me.

On the 8th of July I reached Calcutta, putting up at The Great Eastern Hotel in Old Court House Street. I decided to spend another year running all over India, reserving about three months to settle up some awkward financial transactions in Egypt before going home to England.

Now in Calcutta it is always very hot indeed at this time of the year. The monsoon has not yet broken and the place is oppressive. This periodical South West Wind blows from the Indian Ocean, from May to October, then it seems to all blow back again from the North East during November on to April. Having qualified for a Pilot's Certificate, I am flying a Moth aeroplane over this vast city. It is really an immense place but the good roads are very few and far between and the remainder are not fit for motoring.

We did a tour of the fine shopping centre. I purchased a gold cigarette case for my dad, a black opal for my sister and a sapphire brooch of fine local work for my mother, which I dispatched, just to show that I was still in the land of the living and perhaps hoping that it might partly atone for the absence of letter I should have sent in the past.

I booked up a run on the British India Steam Navigation Company Steam Ship *Angora* from Mandalay via Bangkok to Rangoon (Strand Hotel). I cabled our Manager at Freudenberg and Company, Mont Street, Madras, the Headquarters of the Subsidiary Company which I had floated, when I was on my way up. We had a fine showroom and business was booming.

On my arrival I was pressed in to the ceremony known as the Ayuda Puja where the priests bless the tools, the houses, the carts and the bullocks, and ask for protection and good luck through the coming year. I was a Burra Sahib at this religious festival so they threw in an extra blessing for me and my car.

Christmas 1927 I spent at Maidens Hotel, New Delhi, after completing a great journey, by car, from Bombay. This journey caused quite a stir and the Press took it much to their advantage. I supplied them with photographs and several interviews. It appears the trip had not been done before via Hyderabad and certainly I had cut the time down by several weeks although I had made many calls en route.

We had a grand time over the long Christmas holidays. I joined an elephant shooting party and I got my second tiger early on. Leopard, jackal, buck and a vast variety of birds provide us with plenty of practice.

During Princes' Week I have been rushing around. Every day I am interviewing some of the Royalty and Chiefs of States. Some of the costumes are simply marvellous and must have cost a mint of money. The highly coloured tents and native officers' uniforms add much gaiety to this important function. Shortly the hot season will be upon us here then the Government and others will move up into the Hills of Simla.

April 1928. I am down with fever again and to make a good job of it I have indulged in a motor smash which got my left leg. Anyhow I am full of 'Beans' and hold receptions and interviews most days.

I am reading H.G. Wells' Time Machine. Remembering that he was born in Bromley, Kent, the same as myself, I noted that he mentions a Filby as one of his characters. No doubt he had our family in mind. [Archie is right. H.G. Wells mentions an argumentative young man with red hair, and this was actually Archie himself.]

I quietly looked over my accounts and business expenses. They have now soared to well over £100 per month. Of course every payment is debited to 'business' as agreed. Everyone is satisfied! The city is looking very like England for the men are wearing overcoats and the women their furs of evenings.

ॐ 33 ॐ

INDIA

[Article (dated June, 1928) in the publication INDIAN AND EASTERN MOTORS entitled THE BEAN CAR IN INDIA. It was written by A.E. Filby and the publication describes it as, quote: "...an account by the writer, whose initials thinly disguise a personality well known to the motor trade in the East, of jungle trips taken in a Bean car from end to end of India."]

After a run down towards Trichinopoly and district, which provided some rough going, we set out on a run to Bangalore. The road is for the most part interesting but Fort Round at Veldrome, which is the best route, is of most interest. Bangalore proved to be much cooler than Madras. I was accompanied on this part of the trip by Messrs. Freudenberg and Kenny also Mr. Gay, who were driving an eight-cylinder American car of well-known make. While on this trip I was using a Bean Six. On arrival in Bangalore we stopped at "Jimmy" Lavender's, who, in my opinion, puts up the best food in the East.

The following morning we set off just after day-break and arrived at Mysore for tiffin (tiffin is a snack or light meal). In the evening we had a run round, the zoo proving well worth a visit. Later in the evening we saw a rare sight: The palace which is very beautiful was a blaze of light, while the tops of the hills in the background had their outlines picked out with light. A trip up to the temple which stands on Chahmundi hill above the town was made, and looking down on the city it appeared as if it was built in the water, as the lamp stands are of some white stone which gives a reflection at the base of each.

Leaving Mysore in the morning we soon came to the foot of the Ootacamund ghats (a ghat is a mountain pass). Here I gave the other car about about half an hour's start but caught up to them before they got to the top, the Bean proving fast in third gear and very easy to handle at the sharp corners. Wonderful scenery is to be seen all the way up; the road from above is like some huge serpent climbing the mountain. At the top, the downs remind one of English Moors.

We passed through Ooty and had the pleasure of stopping with a friend of Mr. Kenny's, whose house is one of the highest points, and when we arrived it was wrapped in clouds. A return was started just after breakfast with us nearly freezing to death. I stopped behind to let the other car start the descent of the ghats while we took a little longer route as we wished to make a call. On arrival at the foot, a drink was suggested as we did not think we would be able to catch the other car. As we had just settled down to some beer and sandwiches in the shade of a cool Tamarind tree, who should come on from behind but our friends in the other car. I must admit that I had let the car sail down but it was under perfect control the whole time – they were considerably surprised to see us ahead and a little annoyed, especially as we had made a considerable hole in the provisions. From there on we made a fast run into Bangalore stopping at Mysore for tiffin.

On my return to Madras I picked up the new Hadfield model 14/15 Bean and started off on the run to Delhi accompanied by Mr. and Mrs. Gay and Mr. Bengale, both driving other cars.

The first part of the journey was without incident, a stop being made at Nellore Railway Station for tiffin. The result of the last cyclone in this district was very noticeable, houses had lost their roofs while the road was blocked by huge trees blown across the way which had been sawn through leaving a very narrow path between. We pushed through intent, on reaching Bezwada, which was our destination for the night, after wiring ahead to the station to have the inevitable chicken ready, but we were doomed to be chickenless that night, as just after dark we came on a river which had three feet of water. We retraced our steps a short way and put up for the night in a dâk bungalow.

In the morning we ascertained that we would have to make a detour of 120 miles to reach a spot 30 miles the other side of the river. We had to cross a few small rivers this way, and once one of the cars stuck but got out again under its own power.

At night we had rather an exciting experience crossing the breakwater at Bezwada. We had to run the car on the sloping rubble that formed the back of the dam and this in the dark. All the cars came through O.K. although my boy was convinced that at any moment we should find a watery grave.

A halt was made for the night at the excellent rooms at the station, but we were off agin the following morning after a fill-up which revealed the astonishing fact that Mr. Gay's eight-cylinder was doing 22 m.p.g. while mine was doing nearly 30. That day we encountered several difficult rivers, in one of which all of us stuck in the water and loose sand, but with the help of four bullocks and "umpteen" coolies we got through and arrived that night in Secunderabad after losing our way.

Secunderabad proved to be very interesting, but we were very careful not to go about much as 120 were dying a day from the plague while there were 7,000 people away from the town, which gave the place a very mournful appearance. I saw eight dead bodies during my first trip down town, so decided not to make a long stay.

I parted company with my friends who were returning to Madras, and pushed on to Bombay. Here is where the trouble really started: after a few miles of good running, the road suddenly ceased – on making enquiries I was told that if I kept to the line of cactus trees and kept a certain hill ahead I should eventually strike a good road again – so we pushed on passing through several small villages the inhabitants of which were very interested at the way we were going along over the rough road and assured us we should not get through. I got one of the shepherds to stand on the running board and direct us. Striking a smoother patch I was able to increase speed, when he jumped off rolling head over heels in a mass of whirling pugree, etc.

I went back expecting to see him with his neck broken, but he jumped up quite pleased with his effort and was off back to his village to tell of his experiences. Why cannot all pedestrians be cheerful about it, like this?

We now came to river after river with wonderful bridges over them if they had had any road in the middle; as it was, the centre had fallen through in every case with the result that we had to slide down one bank into the water then get out to find a place to scramble up on the other side. In one case I had to go about three hundred yards up stream to find a bank with a slope that I could get up. After this the road improved a lot but just at sundown we again came to a river which looked at first appearances to be too deep. The scenery here was very pretty, the setting sun lit up the river and a wonderful old fort on its banks. By this time we had nearly run out of petrol and I half expected to run out in mid stream. We however got through okay and were met the other side by the whole of the Customs office staff who seemed surprised to see a car coming from this side. On enquiring for petrol we were told that it should take 24 hours to get some down from Sholapur, so I borrowed kerosene from their lamps and a small extra supply that they had. The car did not seem to notice the change.

We stopped at a really good rest house for the night in Sholapur, up by daylight in the morning, emptied the petrol tank and filled it up with petrol. An uneventful run then to Poona, the car singing along at a nice comfortable speed with the speedometer about 45. The following day I spent in Poona and left about 8-30 p.m. A full moon was shining making the ghats a beautiful sight. To add to this there were several large bush fires which gave the hill a crown of fire.

During the night we had fallen in with dacoits [in India and Burma, a member of a gang of armed robbers] robbing a bullock train and had chased them with the result that my boy "Sammy" was very scared of travelling at night and kept saying "master doesn't know this country, should have a gun." He kept this up for so long that I began to think I should have to have one, especially after we passed a specially happy wedding party. Later on, topping a rise to a bridge, I saw blood pouring down and thought that at last we had struck the real thing and the dacoits had seen our lights approaching and were hiding ready to pounce on us. As it was too late to stop I changed down and raced up with the intention of charging into the waiting dacoits, but on the lights coming to the level of the bridge, discovered a water buffalo with its head practically cut off. From here the descent started; running down, with the car well in hand in third, we made good time over excellent roads, arriving in Bombay at midnight, where we learnt that the ghats were closed after sunset as they were considered too dangerous.

A few days were spent in Bombay and then the journey was continued on to Delhi, the first stop being made at Nasik, the ghats providing beautiful scenery.

Off again the following morning arriving in Mhow just about sunset where I had the pleasure of staying at the excellent club there; the only drawback was the howling of the jackals who had a concert outside my room.

The next day we had an easy run to Gwalior where the night was spent. Here I met a friend who was driving a 3 litre Sunbeam, but as he preferred to travel about 90mph we did not see much of him. There are some wonderful stretches of straight road here and one can go all out. I was very interested in the number of weddings we met, the decorated bullock carts and the bright colours of the people making a very pretty sight, while the guns and swords carried by the mounted men added to their appearance. On this run we had to cross the Tapti River on a craft which would only just take the car, the operation rather resembling a balancing feat. The road is exceptionally dry and dusty there being no green anywhere and hardly any leaves on trees.

A short stay was made at Agra and the famous Taj visited at sunrise, then a quick run to Delhi over excellent roads teeming with blackbuck, deer and peacocks. A few days in Delhi and then a run back to Agra and return to Delhi.

Etawah. - A run out for some shooting again proved that the Bean is the car for real hard work. We used a year old 14 h.p. and left the roads completely. In one case we went up a river bed for about twenty miles, the car pulling excellently in the soft sand. A start was made next day en route – the dust on this run being so bad that on overhauling [overtaking] another car the only means of keeping on the road was to watch the tops of the trees which line it. In the majority of cases the cars overhauled gave up and stopped for the dust to settle. In travelling under these conditions I think an English car driven well will always score as a quick change down to third and one can whip past and gain the clear road ahead.

The following morning about 11, we started for Cawnpore. Arriving there early we stopped till the evening and then pushed on to Lucknow where we stayed the night, and next day from there on through Bebares and Gaya. The road was uninteresting, the Sone river holding us up for four and-a-half hours.

The last day's run of 330 miles proved conclusively that Calcutta has the worst approaches of any town or village in India.

The car finished its run looking as good as when it started.

34

HINDOO

On the Ganges boat, I was annoyed by a fierce looking Hindu who came up from the fourth class, leaving his mob of pilgrims below. They were on their way to participate in a religious festival at Calcutta. The more I moved away from the weird yapping guy, the more he screamed and beseeched me to listen to his pleadings. All the while he suspiciously tapped a mysterious sack.

Into this he thrust his skinny arm and pulled out a young cheetah by the throat. The animal was snarling and snapping its teeth and I was interested. I ordered a steward to put the cheetah into a box and to kick the smelly tramp below or we would chuck him to the crocs in the river.

My latest acquisition was beautiful and I christened him in whisky and named him 'Hindoo'. I had a silver harness made for him and took him about with me. He became greatly attached to me and made a royal guard. Everyone admired him but never too closely.

He also cost me a small fortune in choice meats plus two boys to service him. So when the landlord of the Great Eastern Hotel showed an interest in Hindoo I transferred my pet over to him.

A smart Bentley Tourer swished into the forecourt of the Great Eastern Hotel, Calcutta, discharging a young couple.

"That's Brown, the American multi-millionaire," murmured my chum Ricaldi. "They are doing India and China for their honeymoon."

A few minutes later the young lady stepped across to our lounge and begged to be allowed to pat my beautiful pedigree cheetah which I held on a silver leash.

"What a glorious creature," she exclaimed in adoration, "I would love to have one."

Her husband who was standing within earshot, very politely said to me, "Excuse me, sir, but would you permit me to make an offer to buy him for my wife?"

I just smiled and smoked on.

"What would be your price?" he continued encouragingly.

"Five thousand pounds," I declared very seriously.

"Oh come," said Brown, "he can't be worth all that, eh?"

Over a cigar, the chat turned to river steamers and the 'other matter' was dropped except for a parting remark of the American.

"Glad to meet you, gentlemen, we shall be back sure next week and as you are staying here we will have a chat about 'that'!"

Ten days later the tourists returned from their sight-seeing up the Brahmaputra.

"Good morning, Mr Filby," says Brown, giving me a friendly handshake. "Where's your cheetah today, sold it?"

"Oh yes, for five thousand guineas too," I replied.

"Cashed the cheque?" the American whispered doubtingly.

"Better than that," said I, "I took a pedigree monkey and a lineage prize cat, worth two and a half thousand guineas each in exchange!"

35

SINGAPORE, INDIA, BURMA [MYANMAR], THAILAND AND CHINA

Many were the pleasant evenings we spent in those strenuous days of business and pleasure. It was at Singapore that I won the Federated Malay States High Diving Championship, a great satisfaction to me and indeed no mean achievement. There were many entries including expert native divers. In one test we did a double somersault.

While still in Singapore, I took into partnership (for sporting purposes only) a young Don from Cambridge who was waltzing around the world completing his education.

I had no objection to the terms of fifty-fifty: he did the paying and I did the piloting. For he bought, under my guidance, a de Havilland Moth Seaplane, the Kestrel G-AADK. That was in the Spring 1928. We had some wonderful flights and I kept a clean sheet right through.

As a member of the Singapore Flying Club, I now took a very active part. Aeronautics became an absorbing science with me. I could almost pilot a machine while asleep. My youthful experience in 1917 in The Royal Flying Corps stood me in good stead. That was behind the lines in France and Belgium.

I thought of those rough and ready times - those suicidal contraptions we went up in - in the days of Hope and Glory. The planes of those days were as up to date as the 'Rocket' is to the modern locomotive. They were in fact as childish as I was in 1917. Still I think The Old Rocket had the laugh of us. When the engine conked out it stopped. Not so our splutterer in 1917, for we kept on moving - downwards.

My stunts and ideas were being broadcast round Malay and I was approached by several eminent firms of plane builders, including Shorts and Blackburns Plane and Motor Company, of York. They tried to impress on me that motor cars were a thing of the past. For the present and future it would be planes - just planes.

They initiated me into some of their secrets and we had private demonstrations, often at night. Big money was offered to me to come in but I definitely declined to tie myself up just then.

I got on the move again but before leaving Singapore I sold our dear little Kestrel with misgivings. The new owners were a little unlucky for within 48 hours the joy of our heart had come to a full stop - upside down. And that was the last I saw of the Kestrel.

I travelled thousands of miles through Bombay, Hyderabad, Bengal, Assam, Burma, China, Japan, and Korea.

"Up and down the city road, in and out of the Eagle.

That's the way the money goes - pop goes the weasel!"

I ponder over those last two lines. Money. Money in India. It comes in in chunks and we pour it out like water. As for the suggestion of 'up and down the city road', well, I keep flying, driving, on the train, or ship up and down the universe.

From my log I find I call again at that wonderful public house, The Taj Mahal (Hotel, not the Tomb) in Bombay. I meet Mr Ricardo, the chief of General Motors. He introduces me to everyone worth knowing: Princes, Potentates, and Leaders of Business in the City.

Weeks pass and I am away 'down the city road' to Baroda, Jaipur and new Delhi. Then further north to Simla, skirting Tibet. Working south I make Allahabad and Benares, across to Bengal, stopping at

Calcutta. Shipping across to Rangoon, I stay at The Strand Hotel for a month.

Taking the road to Mandalay, I cross from Burma to Siam [Thailand], with a rest in Bangkok. Now in China, I anchor myself for some weeks in that strange city Shanghai. What a mixture of pomp and poverty, modern elegance and ancient slums.

In Assam I was fortunate to fall in with Mr Mawson of Began Roberts and Company, Leadenhall Street, London. This led to some useful business.

I also did a wild drive away to Kaboo on the Upper Ganges and got away in the mountain passes with the crags towering 15,000 feet above me. Journeys out of Poona, Sura Kothapur, before finally doing Japan and Korea were all part of the curriculum. I felt that a spot of rest was needed.

I had been 'up and down the road, in and out of the Eagle' most certainly. I would take a holiday at home, say ten months, and would saunter round England, Wales and Scotland. That's the way the money goes! With lots of other ways.

Before closing, as this will most likely meet the eye of a friend, I add: my thanks are due to the Officials of the Chartered Bank, Colombo, and Branches. Also the Staff of The Bank of Australasia who were so helpful to me during my five years long tour in the Far East.

(Maybe otherwise I might have added: "Pop goes the weasel.")

Pop is a pledge or pawn. Weasel is a tailor's tool.

Then, through China and a little visit to Mongolia by car, aeroplane, horse, mule, railway and rickshaw.

For some months I made Pekin and Tiensin my centre, staying at The Tudor House Hotel at the latter town, a really first class place.

With a chum I took a 700 mile run by aeroplane to Shansi, then continued over The Great Wall of China into Mongolia. We soon had enough of Gobi and the desolate regions around which we explored by mule train. I sketched a route through Honan, Nanking and down to

Canton and Hong Kong chiefly by mail steamer. Then to that interesting City of Shanghai.

I well remember a little incident at Foochow where I got in with some fellows of The Speed Boats. They were the Government Revenue Preventive Officers. I could see some good sport, not without some serious risk (which they pointed out) if I assisted them just for once. So at daybreak next morning I joined two officers in a small motor boat to outwit the heathen wily Chinese smugglers.

Our captain at once spotted a suspicious native junk, probably loaded with rubber, dope and so on. He said take the tiller quick and put on speed. I just did! We flew across that half mile and landed right on that old junk's deck before I could shut off.

There was a terrible to-do about it all, especially when we found that our engine was disabled. We promised the swearing Chinaman big compensation and payment if he would get us home again and to shut up about it all! So ended my career as His Majesty's Preventive Officer.

Shanghai of Today! Who can Predict the Shanghai of Tomorrow? After several weeks spent at Canton and district, I shipped to Shanghai, breaking my journey at Hong Kong. I was greatly interested in the City of Shanghai, often called the London, or Brussels, of the East. What a cosmopolitan population! I was told that there were four million Chinese, two million Japanese, about 10,000 British and Russians each, with a lesser number of Americans, Germans and French, and a sprinkling of all other nations. The Far East is always inextricably mixed.

I spent several days in the English comfort and luxury of The Shanghai Club and then moved over to the sumptuous Cathay Hotel. Its Cabaret Shows and Dance Floors are equal to any in our European Capitals.

The lively scenes of the leading merchants with their charming ladies might easily be mistaken for the West End of London. Night Life in Shanghai would quite put London in the shade. It is unwise to venture in to the Chinese Native Quarters without a proper escort or recognised guide or you may become one of those 'mysteries' that remain unsolved.

Motoring along the Nanking road, we pass Halls named Le Oiseau

Bleu, Palais de Lune, The Black Cat, The Cassanova etc and their Filipino jazz bands are the equal of any in America. A stroll down the Shanghai Bund brings one to magnificent hotels, shops banks etc, more elaborate than London.

Yet, had we turned the other way on the Bund, we should now be in the picturesque Native Quarters and streets of old bazaars. Now we notice the Wangpoo River stretching away, with its flotilla of straw-mat covered sampans, in which for countless ages, thousands of Chinese are hatched, matched and dispatched. Many of this herd of humanity never once leave the sampans during the whole of their existence.

The life of 'Old China' goes on as in the time of Confucius. During a little flit by aeroplane, I was struck by the immensity of the Great Wall of China. It stretches away for scores of miles, right away up in to the hills and circle back again. The walls are about six yards broad on the top with a buttress each side about four feet high, so making a walk or road. This ponderous erection is used chiefly for military purposes to this very day. They are carefully guarded in most parts and they are a source of mystery. It's hard to say what they hide or contain.

In Shanghai City, Sir Victor Sassoon owns the chief apartment houses, hotels etc, and is indeed the richest landlord there. In the International Settlement, the Japanese influence is constantly increasing and they outnumber the British by ten to one.

The Japanese and Chinese appear to have skirmishes any or every day. These two nations remind me of a pair of high-class football teams with their peculiar mixture of friendship and enmity. They're always out for peace and business and always anxious to do battle. Most of the Europeans take these outbreaks as portending something serious. The newspapers move with the times and on the least provocation they come out with, "Another Great Battle" three times a day.

We were sitting in the veranda of The Astor House Hotel, having a drink and game of cards, when a battle broke out below in the street. The clash of arms and the shouting of the combatants grew louder and louder. It was very annoying. Seeing the head waiter I asked him what he was going to do about the racket below, as though the poor man was to blame. Wait, he said quietly and going on to the steps he clapped his hands and let go some broken English at the strugglers below and told them they would get a thick ear if they did not buzz off with their darned battle. This they promptly did followed by a hail of broken china as a parting gift.

There were much more serious 'scraps' than that, however. But it was marvellous how everyone went about their business or pleasure without damage while a grim sanguinary battle was waging. The Japanese are keenly alive to the future and they are also well prepared.

Should the occasion demand it, the Japanese are ready to run their fleet of battle ships and aeroplanes up the Woosung, where the Wangpoo River meets the Yangtze. Then will the fate of the whole of the Far East (and much of the West) really hang in the balance.

Have you ever considered the Chinese willow pattern on your china?

While on the spot I inspected a china-manufacturing house. This fine translucent porcelain, or earthenware, was first exported from China in the sixteenth century and, among other things, I was told The Story of the Willow Pattern. As it was news to me, maybe it will be news to others. The famous willow pattern enshrines an ancient legend.

A beautiful Chinese girl, Koong-Shee, loved poor Chang instead of the rich man chosen for her. She was banished to a little house at the back of the garden beside whose window was a willow and fruit tree. One fine day, Chang placed a billet doux [love note] in a shell and floated across a lake to Koong. She bade him come and he eloped with her.

As they crossed the bridge, the girl's father caught them. (In the picture the girl is in front with the distaff, Chang has her jewel case and the old man has a whip.) The lovers escaped and would have lived happily ever after if the disappointed suitor had not set fire to their house whereupon they all vanished in flames.

There is a little sonnet:-

[Actually, this is not a sonnet.]

Two doves flying high,
Chinese sampan sailing by,
Weeping willow hanging or'r,
Bridge with three men, if not four,
Chinese temple, here it stands,
Seems to cover all the land.
Here's the tree with apples on,
A pretty ending to my song.

36

THROUGH PERSIA, IRAQ AND BACK TO THE UNITED KINGDOM

Running along the lands of the old Assyrian Empire, I spent some time at Baghdad. Years before I had made a note to remind myself to visit Nimrud (or Nimrad), on the Euphrates, and see for myself the elaborate and wonderful Palace that had so definitely put Nimrud in so exulted a position in the history of the Middle East! But the only Palace I could find was in ruins.

On May 3rd 1929 I sailed from Bombay with the Peninsular and Oriental Steam Navigation Company's Steam Ship *Damola*. The Belgravia Hotel, London, was reached via Marseilles and the overland route. It was altogether a delightful voyage and after I had transacted business in London, Paris and Berlin, I decided to pop down and give the family a surprise and myself a long holiday.

Several weeks later, after several interviews with the Directors of The Bean Car Company, I again sailed East, doing all the principal towns. The chief calls were at Kobe, Canton, Shanghai, Nanking, Peking, Port Arthur, etc. In fact covering China, Japan and Korea thoroughly.

I had a good time at Tiensin, staying at the Tudor House Hotel for six weeks, combining business with a lot of first class sport. I now received news that sent me rushing across India once more. making for

Simla I engaged my old suite of chambers and office at Corstorphans and Falettis Cecil Hotel as of yore.

I discovered things were not going as smoothly as I wished and my next particular call was Hong Kong, later fixing up a passage on the Empress of India for England. It was July 1929 when I wirelessed the Chief Offices of The Bean Car Company stating I was on the way with urgent and important business news.

At our first port of call in England, I landed to an express train to the factory in Tipton. On investigation I discovered that things were not going smoothly with them which accounted for the trouble which had caused delays and difficulties.

Many important changes were taking place in the Firm. My friend, Jack Bean, had gone over to Guys Motors in Wolverhampton in the capacity of Export Director and Mr Dickinson Fletcher was now the Director of The Indian and Eastern Motors of Fenchurch Street, London.

I was asked to undertake the task of clearing up a spot of bother Egypt way, which I agreed to do. I was well known at Cairo, Sudan and Assuit where this business was situated.

At Cairo I called upon my old chum Mr Palliachi who was so pleased to see me that he ordered one of the most elaborate feasts just to celebrate my visit.

Shortly after this I severed my connection with the Enfield Bean Car Company.

In Conclusion

Au revoir to the many, many countries of The Far East - but not goodbye! The six years I spent in The Orient will always be indelibly impressed on my mind's eye. The wonderful native scenes, the strange doctorings, the various religions with their weird ceremonies.

The fabulous wealth of the potentates and the marvellous power and sway of these Rulers over myriads of people always struck me as something uncanny and wonderful. It was pleasant to find that the preponderance of these Rulers are ultra loyal to our King and Country.

The Far East is inexhaustible, whether for arts and crafts, touring, hunting, sight-seeing or business purposes. for those believers in occultism, the investigation of the unknown and mysterious, the supernatural and magic power of theosophy, well, GO EAST!

I shall return again to it all in a few years, with a set purpose of travelling far into the interior, away from the beaten track, over the vast rolling deserts, the forbidding mountain passes, through the unlimited tropical jungles, on and on, until I meet ice and snow.

For nothing seems to sap or cure my horizon fever. To me there is an irresistible pull about India, China, Korea, Mongolia, Tibet; and I shall not resist it!

Truly Asia Calling!

EPILOGUE
A TRAGIC LOVE STORY

Archie, having arrived back in England, was already planning another round trip to Cape Town, again by car, but this time blazing a trail down the west coast of Africa and returning along the east. This he successfully completed and his expedition in a sawn-in-half Model T Ford is described in *Horizon Fever I*.

Ultimately he would cross the Sahara seven times, once on his own.

By now he was quite famous and being heralded as 'the World's most travelled motorist'. He was much in demand on radio and television. In one BBC radio broadcast, 'In Town Tonight', Mrs Patricia Byron, another globe-trotter, described a dramatic rescue. She was stranded in the heart of the Sahara, an area larger than the United States, and two hundred miles from the nearest town. Whether or not she was alone is uncertain. Suddenly, through the heat-haze, a decrepit motor vehicle appeared, manned by a sand-and-wind swept individual. He repaired her radiator, allowing her to continue her journey, and frankly saved her life. It was none other than my Uncle Archie.

A week later, and by popular demand, Archie appeared again on the same BBC radio programme. One listener, Miss Fay Taylor, recognised the voice of a man she had met in the Far East, twelve years earlier, when she was a girl of sixteen. It was by chance that Fay heard the broadcast, having been stung by a bee, and changing her plans, had stayed at home. She telephoned the BBC and she and Archie met up again. They renewed their friendship, which blossomed into romance, and were married in Kingston, Surrey, on the 7th October 1938.

Both Fay and Archie were now invited to relate their story on BBC Radio and Television.

In 1939, Archie and Fay continued travelling abroad together, until September, when World War II broke out. Both applied to work in any capacity designated by the War Office and both were posted to Iceland. In 1941, Archie successfully applied for a transfer to West Africa, an area he was intimate with. Fay would follow him after a three-month ship voyage, via Canada and the United States.

Arriving at Freetown, Sierra Leone, Uncle Archie assumed his duties at the British Naval Base. Whilst waiting for Fay, he narrowly missed seeing his younger brother, my father, who was being transported to Burma and whose ship was one of many moored in the Freetown harbour. Archie commandeered a rowing boat and made a valiant but unsuccessful attempt to find his younger brother. They never saw each other again.

Disaster struck. Already prone to recurring bouts of malaria, Archie succumbed to one final violent attack. He fell into a coma from which he never recovered and died on 8 October 1942.

He was 42 years old. Fay arrived in Freetown one day too late.

Fay stayed on at the Naval Base. In a final family volume, Archie's father briefly mentions that Fay re-married "at a little old church, Freetown" in 1945, but to whom, and what became of the couple, is not known.

A REQUEST...

If you enjoyed this book, I'd be so grateful if you left an Amazon review, even if it's simply one sentence.

THANK YOU!

SO WHAT HAPPENED NEXT?

Horizon Fever III - Seven Crossings of the Sahara Desert

Archibald Edmund Filby's account, with photographs, of his seven extraordinary crossings of the Sahara desert, one of which he completed alone.

If you would like advance notice of when this book is published, or would like to contact us with comments or questions, please subscribe to our newsletter at www.victoriatwead.com.

Or email us at TopHen@VictoriaTwead.com.

We'd love to hear from you!

ABOUT VICTORIA TWEAD

Victoria Twead is the founder of Ant Press which has been involved with publishing memoirs since 2011.

After living in a remote mountain village in Spain for eleven years, and owning probably the most dangerous cockerel in Europe, Victoria and her husband, Joe, retired to Australia where another joyous life-chapter has begun.

Victoria is the New York Times bestselling author of *Chickens, Mules and Two Old Fools* and the subsequent books in the Old Fools series. Her days are now spent adding to the Old Fools series, helping authors publish their own memoirs and playing Princesses with her granddaughters.

Email: TopHen@VictoriaTwead.com (emails welcome)
Website: www.VictoriaTwead.com
Old Fools' updates Signup: www.VictoriaTwead.com
This includes the latest Old Fools' news, free books, book recommendations, and recipe. Guaranteed spam-free and sent out every few months.
Free Stuff: http://www.victoriatwead.com/Free-Stuff/

Facebook: https://www.facebook.com/VictoriaTwead (friend requests welcome)
Instagram: @victoria.twead
Twitter: @VictoriaTwead
Patreon: https://www.patreon.com/VictoriaTwead

We Love Memoirs

Join Victoria and other memoir authors and readers in the We Love Memoirs Facebook group, the friendliest group on Facebook.
www.facebook.com/groups/welovememoirs/

ANT PRESS BOOKS
AWESOME AUTHORS - AWESOME BOOKS

If you enjoyed this book, you may also enjoy these Ant Press titles:

MEMOIRS

Dear Fran, Love Dulcie: Life and Death in the Hills and Hollows of Bygone Australia collated by Victoria Twead

Chickens, Mules and Two Old Fools by Victoria Twead (Wall Street Journal Top 10 bestseller)
Two Old Fools - Olé! by Victoria Twead
Two Old Fools on a Camel by Victoria Twead (thrice New York Times bestseller)
Two Old Fools in Spain Again by Victoria Twead
Two Old Fools in Turmoil by Victoria Twead
Two Old Fools Down Under by Victoria Twead
One Young Fool in Dorset (Prequel) by Victoria Twead
One Young Fool in South Africa (Prequel) by Joe and Victoria Twead
Two Old Fools Boxset, Books 1-3 by Victoria Twead

Fat Dogs and French Estates - Part I by Beth Haslam
Fat Dogs and French Estates - Part II by Beth Haslam
Fat Dogs and French Estates - Part III by Beth Haslam
Fat Dogs and French Estates - Part IV by Beth Haslam
Fat Dogs and French Estates - Part V by Beth Haslam
Fat Dogs and French Estates - Boxset, Parts 1-3 by Beth Haslam

From Moulin Rouge to Gaudi's City by EJ Bauer
From Gaudi's City to Granada's Red Palace by EJ Bauer

South to Barcelona: A New Life in Spain by Vernon Lacey

Simon Ships Out: How One Brave, Stray Cat Became a Worldwide Hero by Jacky Donovan
Smoky: How a Tiny Yorkshire Terrier Became a World War II American Army Hero, Therapy Dog and Hollywood Star by Jacky Donovan
Smart as a Whip: A Madcap Journey of Laughter, Love, Disasters and Triumphs by Jacky Donovan

Midwife: A Calling by Peggy Vincent
Midwife: A Journey by Peggy Vincent
Midwife: An Adventure by Peggy Vincent

Heartprints of Africa: A Family's Story of Faith, Love, Adventure, and Turmoil by Cinda Adams Brooks
How not to be a Soldier: My Antics in the British Army by Lorna McCann
Moment of Surrender: My Journey Through Prescription Drug Addiction to Hope and Renewal by Pj Laube

One of its Legs are Both the Same by Mike Cavanagh
A Pocket Full of Days, Part 1 by Mike Cavanagh
A Pocket Full of Days, Part 2 by Mike Cavanagh

Horizon Fever by A E Filby
Horizon Fever 2 by A E Filby

Completely Cats - Stories with Cattitude by Beth Haslam and Zoe Marr

Fresh Eggs and Dog Beds: Living the Dream in Rural Ireland by Nick Albert
Fresh Eggs and Dog Beds 2: Still Living the Dream in Rural Ireland by Nick Albert
Fresh Eggs and Dog Beds 3: More Living the Dream in Rural Ireland by Nick Albert

Fresh Eggs and Dog Beds 4: More Living the Dream in Rural Ireland by Nick Albert

Don't Do It Like This: How NOT to move to Spain by Joe Cawley, Victoria Twead and Alan Parks

Longing for Africa: Journeys Inspired by the Life of Jane Goodall. Part One: Ethiopia by Annie Schrank
Longing for Africa: Journeys Inspired by the Life of Jane Goodall. Part Two: Kenya by Annie Schrank

A Kiss Behind the Castanets: My Love Affair with Spain by Jean Roberts
Life Beyond the Castanets: My Love Affair with Spain by Jean Roberts

The Sunny Side of the Alps: From Scotland to Slovenia on a Shoestring by Roy Clark

FICTION

Parched by Andrew C Branham

A is for Abigail by Victoria Twead (Sixpenny Cross 1)
B is for Bella by Victoria Twead (Sixpenny Cross 2)
C is for the Captain by Victoria Twead (Sixpenny Cross 3)
D is for Dexter by Victoria Twead
The Sixpenny Cross Collection, Vols 1-3 by Victoria Twead

NON FICTION

How to Write a Bestselling Memoir by Victoria Twead
Two Old Fools in the Kitchen, Part 1 by Victoria Twead

CHILDREN'S BOOKS

Seacat Simon: The Little Cat Who Became a Big Hero by Jacky Donovan
Morgan and the Martians by Victoria Twead

LARGE PRINT BOOKS

Chickens, Mules and Two Old Fools by Victoria Twead (Wall Street Journal Top 10 bestseller)
Two Old Fools - Olé! by Victoria Twead
Two Old Fools on a Camel by Victoria Twead (thrice New York Times bestseller)
Two Old Fools in Spain Again by Victoria Twead
Two Old Fools in Turmoil by Victoria Twead
Two Old Fools Down Under by Victoria Twead
One Young Fool in Dorset (The Prequel) by Victoria Twead
One Young Fool in South Africa (The Prequel) by Joe and Victoria Twead
Fat Dogs and French Estates - Part I by Beth Haslam
Fat Dogs and French Estates - Part II by Beth Haslam
Fat Dogs and French Estates - Part III by Beth Haslam
Fat Dogs and French Estates - Part IV by Beth Haslam
A Kiss Behind the Castanets: My Love Affair with Spain by Jean Roberts

ANT PRESS ONLINE

Why not check out Ant Press's online presence and follow our social media accounts for news of forthcoming books and special offers?

Website: www.antpress.org
Email: admin@antpress.org
Facebook: www.facebook.com/AntPress
Instagram: www.instagram.com/publishwithantpress
Twitter: www.twitter.com/Ant_Press

HAVE YOU WRITTEN A BOOK?

Would you love to see your book published? Ant Press can help! Take a look at www.antpress.org or contact Victoria directly.

Email: TopHen@VictoriaTwead.com

www.ingramcontent.com/pod-product-compliance
Lightning Source LLC
Chambersburg PA
CBHW060047230426
43661CB00004B/683